# Full Circle

A Life of Fishing and Adventure

# Full Circle

## A Life of Fishing and Adventure

David Van Lear, Ph.D.

PALMETTO
PUBLISHING
Charleston, SC
www.PalmettoPublishing.com

Copyright © 2024 by David Van Lear

All rights reserved

No portion of this book may be reproduced, stored in a retrieval system, or transmitted in any form by any means–electronic, mechanical, photocopy, recording, or other–except for brief quotations in printed reviews, without prior permission of the author.

Hardcover ISBN: 979-8-8229-3941-7
Paperback ISBN: 979-8-8229-3942-4

# Acknowledgements

Many people contributed to the experiences that have made these stories possible. I owe a special thanks to friends who fished with me and occasionally "fished" me out of rivers! I will never forget my fishing friends. You made my life richer and more interesting. I also want to thank friends who encouraged me to tell my tales.

I must also thank the wonderful Certified Nursing Assistants (CNAs) who work at Clemson Downs where my wife and I live. They do so much more than just bring me medications every day; they help me with my computer ineptitude, a problem that raises its head almost daily for me. Without their help, I would never have been able to complete this book of short stories, nor my previous book Turning Points in the Life of a Fisherman. No matter how insignificant you thought your assistance was, your help made the difference that enabled me to complete this little book.

There were many more CNAs who helped me in various ways, but these CNAs in particular provided a great deal of computer assistance. Thanks to all of you: Katia, Shelby, Caroline, Olivia, Lex,

Emily Ann, Zoe, Madison and Kennedy. Each of you is not only sweet and caring to this old man, but so helpful as well. You lifted my spirits every day.

A special thanks to my fishing buddy, former student and great friend, Rick Myers, who graciously gave up his valuable time to write a foreward for this little book. Once again, he has proven to be the kind of guy you want beside you whether you are in the forest, a trout stream or just heading through life. Thank you, Rick.

I owe so much to my book editor, Joquita Burka. She took my best efforts and turned them into much better English and even better context. Thank you so much, Joquita. You were wonderful to work with.

David Van Lear, Ph.D.

# Contents

| | |
|---|---|
| Acknowledgements | vii |
| Foreword | 1 |
| A Float Trip to Remember | 5 |
| Rivers Shaped My Life | 15 |
| Fishing: My Life-Long Addiction | 37 |
| A Grizzly Encounter | 51 |
| Turn Around! | 59 |
| Fishing Adventures with Doc and Willy | 63 |
| Semi-Invalid to Active Old Man | 67 |
| You Can Go Home Again | 75 |
| Splash | 85 |
| Stuck!! | 93 |
| An Old-Timers Love Story | 101 |
| The Incredible Story of Mary Draper Ingles | 111 |
| The Power of Conservation | 121 |
| A Day on the Soque | 131 |

# Foreword

I've known David Van Lear for a long time and was more than a little honored when he asked me to write some opening lines for his new book. Having no experience in writing book forewords, I decided to go looking for some examples. As good fortune would have it, I reached first for About Trout by Robert J. Behnke, with a foreword by the venerable Ted Williams. Williams opens with the phrase, "I wish I'd had Bob Behnke for a professor," and then acknowledges that Dr. Behnke — through his prolific research and influential writing — has served indirectly as a professor to many who care deeply for trout and salmon, and for their conservation.

Unlike Ted Williams I don't have to make a similar wish because I did indeed have David Van Lear as a college professor — first during my years as a forestry undergrad at Clemson, later as a master's student in his advanced silviculture class and finally with him as major advisor for my doctoral degree program. Over the past four decades, Dr. Van Lear has been among my most effective teachers and mentors. He has influenced my outlook on many aspects of life including forest resource conservation, trout fishing and living honorably — which is difficult for us fishermen, but we can try. Now retired from a 40-plus-year career in conservation, I'm fortunate to count him as a close friend and call him Dave. I know that more than a few of his past colleagues and former students share a similar affection for this knowledgeable and decent man.

David Van Lear's career as a forest scientist centered on improving forest management practices to reduce soil and nutrient losses, maintain site productivity, protect stream water quality and conserve biodiversity. The diversity of story subjects in Full Circle reveals his many other interests, including an enduring affection for a wonderful woman named Carolyn, his admiration for an ancestor who persevered against all odds, his appreciation for friends and caregivers, and his deep belief in the value of public lands such as the Clemson Experimental Forest.

On the surface some of these chapters appear to be about fishing; however, you will discover that they are much more than that. Yes, there are some yarns about big fish, somewhat-hard-to believe situations, perhaps some exaggeration — of course! Van Lear is a fisherman, after all. But importantly for all of us, Dave makes the clear case that fishing expeditions can be more than just a form of recreation. Indeed, they are a means of learning about the natural world and about oneself. Perhaps most significantly, he suggests that fishing can be a kind of coping mechanism, helping us deal with some of the more difficult aspects of living — specifically, the maintenance of mental health. I so very much relate to this thesis, because for most of my life the fishing and hunting trips on my calendar provided an unending series of wonderful things to look forward to, improving my state of mind. Dave's examples in Full Circle strongly support the notion that pending adventures can serve as tonic, reduce mild depression and help us through life's challenges, concerns and drudgeries.

Fishing as therapy makes a lot of sense, and I'm certain that Dave is onto something here. Whether solo or with friends, fishing — as well as other outdoor pursuits — immerses us in nature, taking our focus away from the daily grind. Shared experiences with a close fishing partner or experienced guide promote insight and idea sharing. And then, there's the fact that it's extremely enjoyable to hook and play a fish — as summarized by a current popular phrase among fishers: "The tug is the drug."

In addition to his prolific writing, another of Dave's great lifetime contributions has been his influence on hundreds of college students over a long career of classroom teaching. He has also mentored graduate students in research methods and conveyed information to colleagues and peers via professional conference presentations. Dave's gentle nature, expertise and preparation make it easy to listen to him and believe the ideas he shares. He's long been the consummate educator.

While reading Full Circle, I know that you'll appreciate Dave's sincerity, earnestness, good humor and honesty (except about the fishing stuff) as much as I have. If you already know him well, then like me you are already an admirer of his ardent love and devotion to fishing, friends, family and conservation. Or, if you are just meeting him for the first time through these chapters, I assure you that he is just as authentic and earnest and kind as he appears to be through his writing. I'm so glad you got to meet him!

Rick Myers  *December 2023*

# A FLOAT TRIP TO REMEMBER

When I was a junior in high school, my friend, Jimmy Durvin, and I decided to take a float trip down a 20-mile stretch of the Cowpasture River outside Clifton Forge, Virginia. Float trips on the Cowpasture River of that length were unheard of back in the mid-1950s, but we had been reading articles in outdoor magazines about float fishing on rivers in the Ozarks. It seemed logical to our young minds, that the Cowpasture would be a good river to float as well.

In our plan, my dad would drive us up-river to Camp Mont Shenandoah early one July morning, and we would float, paddle and fish for two days, spending one night somewhere on the river — we had no idea where — and hopefully arrive at my folks' cabin on the banks of the Cowpasture on the evening of the second day. Simple, right?

My parents were certainly a little apprehensive about our grandiose plans, but they were always willing to let their children live out their dreams, a trust for which I have always been grateful.

Before Jimmy and I left for our adventure, we decided to do a trial run, and it's a good thing we did! The two of us loaded Dad's 10-foot wooden pram with all our gear (sleeping bags, food, fishing rods, tackle boxes, a bundle of firewood, and one tarp to serve as our tent and another to cover our supplies) and pushed out into the calm eddy in front of my family's cabin on the banks of the river. But the boat could hardly hold it all, and the gunwales were barely above water when Jimmy and I climbed in. No doubt, we would have sunk in the first substantial rapids we encountered.

The boat just wasn't big enough. So, we decided to make a floating storage platform from a sheet of plywood tied to two large truck-tire innertubes. We attached the raft to the back of the boat with a four-foot-long piece of nylon rope and loaded our supplies on it. It seemed to work, at least to us, so now we had the storage needed to carry our supplies.

Jimmy spent the night before our big adventure with me at the cabin. Early the next morning we loaded the boat and raft into the back of Dad's grocery-store delivery truck and headed up-river along Route 42 to our put-in spot at Camp Mont Shenandoah.

What a scene it was — Jimmy and I pushing that little pram out into a calm eddy of the river with our makeshift raft full of supplies tied to the back of the boat while Dad watched nervously from the bank, knowing that no one floated the Cowpasture back in those days, especially for 20 miles. Dad had a right to be apprehensive.

"We'll see you and Mom tomorrow evening," I confidently called out to Dad as we paddled out into the river. "Don't worry, we'll be fine."

"Please be careful," Dad hollered back.

As Dad got in his truck and began slowly driving away, Jimmy and I looked at each other with mixed emotions — excitement and apprehension. We were now on our own, off on a great adventure. We were adventurous, but so naïve. What lay ahead of us? I had fished parts of the river with Dad and knew what those parts were like, but we also knew that there were riffles, even rapids, on the river that we had never seen and that might be dangerous.

*The eddy in front of my parent's cabin where we made our test run before heading out on our big adventure*

While it seemed to us that we were in a very remote location, the river was paralleled by a highway that ran from a quarter- to half-mile away. In fact, we would occasionally hear traffic when the road wound even closer. But along the Cowpasture in 1957, there were few summer cabins. There were occasional farms, but few cabins along most of the river. To us, we were all alone on the river. Although we had been floating and fishing for hours, we had not seen another person all day.

Jimmy was what you might call "a big ol' boy," about 250 pounds, and it wasn't all muscle, if you get my meaning. The sides of our little boat extended only three or four inches above the water level when we were on board. If we simply leaned to one side too much, water would pour in. "Oh my gosh," I thought. "Don't let us flip over!"

However, in our bravado, we thought that if we did flip over, we shouldn't be in too much danger since I was a good swimmer and Jimmy a good floater.

About 11 o'clock that morning, we came out of a riffle into a long smooth eddy. We had been catching some fish, mostly small bass and bluegills, when we suddenly saw a small minnow skipping along the surface with a nice bass chasing after it. They were about 100 feet below us. I was casting a small Abu-Garcia spinning lure with an orange body and a black revolving blade with yellow spots.

Jimmy yelled, "Quick, Dave! Cast down there."

He didn't have to tell me twice. I stood up in the boat and let loose with a mighty cast. But the lure never reached its destination. I heard a sickening whack and turned around to see my lure hanging from the middle of Jimmy's forehead.

Jimmy had a stunned look on his face, and said, "What the hell happened?"

I scrambled to the back of the boat where Jimmy was sitting. Thankfully, the hooks of the lure had not penetrated beyond the barbs, and I was able to easily back the hooks out. We sat there for a minute, thinking how fortunate we were that the lure had not hooked Jimmy in the eye or lip. My foolish cast could have cost him his eye, and I would never have forgiven myself for my stupid mistake.

We recovered, and soon we were paddling again. Jimmy, one of the most even-tempered persons I knew, never even brought the incident up again. But to me the whole event just emphasized the dangers of being young and foolish. I knew a more mature person would not have made that mistake. How do young people make it to adulthood?

That afternoon, after we had floated maybe six or eight miles, a strong thunderstorm blew up suddenly. I told Jimmy, "Let's row to the bank and wait out the storm under that large sycamore hanging over the water. This probably won't last more than a few minutes. Just a summer thunderstorm."

As it turned out, I wasn't much of a weatherman.

Two hours later, the "brief" shower finally quit. It had been more of a "frog strangler" than a gentle summer shower. We had taken shelter under one of the tarps, and as we peeked out, we saw that the other tarp, the one covering our supplies on the raft, had been partially blown off during the storm. Our sleeping bags were as soaking wet as we were. It was not going to be a fun night.

We started to float again, but by now, it was getting late in the evening and, as we fished, we looked for a dry, well-drained, relatively level spot where we could set up camp. Darn, those types of sites were few and far between after that soaking rain. Every potential spot that we inspected was either too brushy, too rocky or too snaky.

Time was running out; it would be night soon. We had to find a spot or darkness would be upon us. And the river was rising and getting muddy!

Finally, as we rounded a bend in the river, we saw an old swinging bridge over the river. No houses were in sight, but we heard a dog bark when our paddle banged on the bottom of the boat. There must be people living nearby, we thought, although their house was not visible from the river.

"Jimmy," I said. "Let's get out and check out this old bridge. It's got to be drier than the spots we've looked at." So, we paddled over to the bank, got out of the boat, and climbed the eight to 10 steps up to the bridge.

"Well, this looks like our best choice yet, Jimmy," I said. "Why don't you clean some of the fish, and I'll make a fire and cut up some potatoes. We'll eat fried fish and potatoes tonight."

Jimmy ambled down to the boat and began pulling up our stringer of fish that we had tied to the back of the boat.

"Good God Almighty!" Jimmy yelled. A huge snapping turtle was eating our fish, and it wasn't about to let go. Its huge head was just inches from Jimmy's hand when he was pulling up the fish stringer. Finally, after I had whacked it on the head several times with a paddle, the monster let go and sank into the depths of the river, leaving behind a scared Jimmy who swore that the turtle almost grabbed his hand when he reached for the stringer.

Good golly! What other surprises would we be in for on this adventure down the river?

"Let's lay out our sleeping bags up on the bridge. At least, we won't have to worry about snakes crawling up beside us," I suggested. So we did, and after eating a couple of soggy peanut butter and jelly sandwiches that mom had packed for us, we lit our Coleman lantern and crawled into our still-wet sleeping bags.

The light from the lantern was comforting at first, but it soon attracted mosquitos and Dobson flies — huge flying insects four- or five-inches long that could draw blood out of you. We finally turned the lantern off and pulled our wet sleeping bags up around our heads. Unfortunately, it was too warm for that, so we yanked our sleeping bags back and endured a night of mosquito bites, the likes of which we had never seen.

It was a night of fitful sleep, if we ever, in fact, fell asleep. Owls were hooting, katydids and cicadas were making their strange sounds, bullfrogs were croaking and mosquitos were buzzing. Several times, the old swinging bridge creaked. Was something coming to get us? A more miserable night I could not imagine.

As dawn was breaking, we were jarred upright by the sound of heavy footsteps on the bridge. We sat up and, peering through the mist and the fog rising from the river, saw a lone figure coming toward us. As he got closer, we could tell it was an old man, dressed in bib overalls, a work shirt, and a baseball hat — a farmer.

"What are you boys doing out here on my bridge?" he bellowed.

"N-N-Nothing," I stammered back, afraid he was going to jump on us for using his bridge. "We were just looking for a dry place to sleep, mister, and this was the best we could find. We were floating down the river to my parent's place below Sharon."

"Well, that's OK. You ain't hurting nuthin'. I'll just step around you, and I'll be on my way. I'm going out to the store that's about a quarter mile out this gravel road, out by the highway, to get my morning paper. Y'all be careful," he said.

As he walked past us, Jimmy and I looked at each other. We were both thinking the same thing.

"Jimmy, maybe we should call it quits," I reasoned. "The river is high and muddy after that big rain yesterday. The fishing probably won't be good, and the river will be more dangerous for us to float. I don't think it would be worth the risk to continue on."

Jimmy didn't need much convincing. He said, "I'm with you. You think your dad would come get us?"

We walked out to the little store the old man had mentioned. It was a typical mid-1950s country store, covered with weathered gray boards to which were attached Martha White Flour, RC Cola and other advertising signs. It was right by the highway. We went in and asked the owner if I could use his phone to call my dad to come pick us up. I said we would pay him for the call — no cell phones back in those days, of course.

He asked who my dad was, and when I told him, he said, "Sure, I know Ed." He pointed me to the phone, and I dialed our camp phone number. It was only about seven in the morning so I knew Dad would not have gone to work yet since he didn't open his store until eight. When Dad answered, I blurted out that we were ready to end our float trip.

*A sketch of the old swinging bridge that Jimmy and I slept on during our 1957 float trip down the Cowpasture River. The drawing was memorialized on a shirt offered by the Cowpasture River Preservation Association (CRPA).*
*Artist: Peggy Terrell*

*Same location, but a newer and sturdier foot bridge across the river. Griffith's Knob is in the background. Photo courtesy of the CRPA.*

"I kind of expected to be getting this call," he said. "We had a downpour here yesterday too, so I thought the river would be getting up and muddy."

"Well, where are you?" he asked. I told him about the little store. He said he knew where it was and would be there in less than a half-hour. He was.

So ended our misadventure of floating down the beautiful Cowpasture River. I don't really know how youngsters make it through their teenage years. We make mistakes (hopefully not tragic ones) and learn from them (hopefully). For Jimmy and me a lot went wrong, but even more could have gone wrong, and it was one heck of an adventure for two 16-year-old hillbillies. I wouldn't trade those memories for anything.

## RIVERS SHAPED MY LIFE

*David Van Lear*

Unlike the central characters in Norman Maclean's brilliant little book, A River Runs Through It, whose lives were shaped by a single river, mine has been shaped by multiple rivers. More accurately, my experiences on a number of rivers have helped shape who I am today.

My passion for rivers and fly fishing started early in my childhood and has continued throughout my life, giving me wonderful adventures and great friends, while helping me cope with cyclothymia, a mild form of bipolar disorder. Without these rivers and the fishing opportunities they provided, I'm sure my life would have been quite different.

While many rivers and creeks played lesser roles in feeding my "addiction" to fishing, these few were the most influential in developing my early love of the sport of fishing.

### The Cowpasture River

The river that gave me my first taste of the joys of fishing was the Cowpasture River, a beautiful clear, cool-water stream that flows for almost 85 miles in the Allegheny Mountains of Virginia. When I was 12 years old, my dad bought two acres along the river from a farmer named Charlie Nicely. My dad owned and operated a small grocery store in Clifton Forge, Virginia, and after work every day, he helped build a cabin for our family on the property. We lived in that cabin from early June when school was out through late fall when cold weather drove us back into town.

I fished and swam in the Cowpasture River almost every day during those summers, and it was there, in 1952 when I was in the eighth grade, that I caught my first large smallmouth bass — a three pounder — in front of our cabin. My memory of that bass is as clear today as it was almost 70 years ago, not only because the catch was a large bass for the river but also because I caught it through sheer luck.

I was in Dad's jon-boat fishing with spring lizards for bait when I had a nibble. I let the fish run with the bait until it stopped, just as Dad had taught me. I struck, but nothing was there. This happened several times, so I figured it must be a small panfish, a bluegill or redeye that was just too little to swallow the bait.

I decided that the next time the fish nibbled I would strike right away rather than letting it run. Maybe I could hook it that way. On my next cast, a fish nibbled again. I struck, and as the small fish was being jerked through the water, there was a sudden strong tug and surprisingly, I was hooked to a much bigger fish!

It was a large smallmouth bass, and it began stripping line off my Johnson Century spincast reel. I had never had that happen before! Then the fish jumped about 10 feet from the boat, scaring the hell out of me. Gradually, I worked it near the boat. Then I did something that was just plain stupid (but I was only 12 years old, so maybe I can be forgiven). I lifted the fish from the water with my rod instead of grabbing it by its lower jaw while it was still in the water. As I tried to swing the fish into the boat, it jerked loose from the hook and, thankfully, landed in the bottom of the boat. I was on it in a flash.

Back in the 1950s, writers in outdoor hunting and fishing magazines, such as Jason Lucas of Sports Afield, (he smoked a pipe and fished for bass with a fly rod, both of which I aspired to do one day) recommended grasping the bass by the lower jaw to land the fish. These guys were my idols, and I recall that they suggested that pressure on the lower jaw would pretty much immobilize the fish, making them easy to land.

Today, tournament fishermen in their haste to land fish as quickly as possible, routinely slide fish rapidly across the surface of the water and in the same motion lift them onto the decks of their bass boats with their rods. But back in 1952, I was no tournament fisherman, and my boat was neither shiny nor did it have a sloping deck.

Landing that bass was pure luck, but I was proud of that fish. It sowed the seeds of my early love for fishing, a love that turned into a positive addiction that has lasted a lifetime.

Ten years later, in the eddy above our Cowpasture River cabin, I caught a 4¼-pound smallmouth bass using a cat minnow, or "mad tom" as we called them, our favorite bait for catching large smallmouth. That was the biggest I caught in those early years of fishing on the Cowpasture while my dad landed the largest catch, a 4¾ pounder nearer our cabin.

*The Cowpasture River in front of our cabin where I caught my first large, smallmouth bass in 1952. The stunning beauty and tranquility of the Cowpasture River hooked me on fishing and nature.*

If my first large, smallmouth bass had landed back in the river instead of in the bottom of my boat, would I have become a serious fisherman? I'm not sure, but that big bass certainly began my addiction to the sport.

Growing up on the Cowpasture taught me to appreciate the beauty of nature and the wonders of a clean, unspoiled river so unlike the nearby Jackson River flowing through Clifton Forge that had been heavily polluted with effluent from a pulp and paper company upstream. Memories of the clear waters of the Cowpasture, and later the rivers of Yellowstone National Park, played major roles in shaping my desire to work in a natural resource field and led to my choice of forestry as my profession.

## THE STREAMS OF YELLOWSTONE NATIONAL PARK

Fishing the Cowpasture in my early years led me to my next big river adventure. I went west to work as a cabin boy at Old Faithful Camper Cabins in Yellowstone National Park in 1958 when I was 17 years old. I had just graduated from high school when my best friend Richard Deeds and I, with the encouragement of my brother Eddy and the somewhat apprehensive endorsement of our parents, got on a train in Clifton Forge, Virginia, and made the three-day journey to Yellowstone. Eddy had worked in Yellowstone the previous summer and told me it would change my life. Was he ever right about that!

I would go on to work four more summers in Yellowstone as a bellhop at Old Faithful and Canyon Village, primarily motivated by my love of the rivers. During those five summers, I came to appreciate that Yellowstone had some of the best trout fishing in the country.

What a stroke of good fortune it was to work in the park within reach of several world-famous trout streams and one not-so-famous creek. During my first summer in the park, Richard and I could walk from our barracks to a beautiful meadow stream named Iron Creek that flowed through Black Sand geyser basin on its way to the Firehole River. I became a serious trout fisherman because of this little creek.

## Iron Creek

During our first few weeks in the park, Richard and I couldn't catch fish on the famous Firehole River because it was restricted to fly fishing only. We were truly disappointed because trout fishing was the primary reason we had come to Yellowstone. We had even seen trout rising in the Firehole River as we approached Old Faithful when we first entered the park from Livingston, Montana, after our long train trip from Virginia.

But we just weren't fly fishermen. We had tried fly fishing but, sad to say, we came up empty most times.

Still, we wanted to fish. In desperation, we asked an old gentleman who worked in the fishing department at the Old Faithful Hamilton Store if he knew of any nearby streams — we didn't own a car — where we could fish with our spinning outfits. That old man saved our summer when he told us about Iron Creek which was just a 15-minute walk through the woods from our barracks at Old Faithful. He said he had fished it years earlier, and back then it had a good population of brown and rainbow trout, plus a few brookies in its upper reaches.

Richard and I were in fishing heaven. The creek flowed through sagebrush and steppe meadows with tongues of lodgepole forests occasionally approaching the water's edge. It was loaded with trout, and we seldom saw another fisherman. We seemed to be the only ones fishing it. Most of Iron Creek between Black Sand and Biscuit basins was far enough away from park roads to feel like a pristine wilderness stream to us.

We caught lots of 10- to 16-inch trout, mostly browns, on spinners and small Rapalas, but one particular trout is burned in my memory. I was fishing about 100 yards downstream from Richard when I heard him yelling as he was running toward me. As he got closer, I saw what had made him so excited — the head and tail of a large trout was sticking out opposite ends of his willow creel!

"Good gosh, Richard. What a trout!" I shouted in disbelief as he pulled the huge brown trout out of his creel and held it up for me to admire. "Wow, that is a monster!" It was the largest trout either of us had ever seen.

He told me he caught it from a pool in the middle of Black Sand Basin where boiling hot water poured into the creek from nearby geysers. He showed me the exact spot as we headed back to our barracks at Old Faithful. I couldn't believe that trout could live in water that I assumed would be too warm. Obviously, I was wrong on that!

We rushed back to the Hamilton store to show the old man our prize catch. He was delighted to see us and weighed and measured Richard's trout. It was 22-inches long and weighed exactly four pounds, by far the biggest trout we caught that golden summer of 1958.

That summer of fishing almost exclusively on Iron Creek hooked me on trout fishing. Over the next four summers that I worked in the park I gradually became not only more addicted to fishing but began trying to fly fish for trout. Although Iron Creek remained one of my favorite streams in Yellowstone, I was no longer limited to just fishing this small creek. By my third summer, I had a car so I was able to explore and fish the more famous streams in Yellowstone.

## The Firehole River

The Firehole River is a world-famous trout stream, totally contained in Yellowstone National Park. It flows through several geyser basins where hot water from boiling springs flows directly into the river. The most famous geyser in the park, Old Faithful, sits in the Upper Geyser Basin alongside the river. It erupts at roughly hourly intervals and discharges thousands of gallons of boiling hot water into the Firehole River.

One experience on the Firehole cemented my love of fly fishing. In 1960, my third summer working in the park, I was attempting to fly fish (I use the term loosely, because I was still a novice to be sure) along a stretch of the river just upstream from Biscuit Basin. An older gentleman was fly fishing in the riffle-run ahead of me. As I watched him making short delicate casts directly upstream of his position, he caught and released two nice trout in just a few minutes. I had never watched an expert fly fisherman practice his skill at such a close range.

Standing there in awe, I suddenly heard and saw a splashy rise in a slough on the other side of the river. As I gazed intently at the riseform, I noticed a couple of dragonflies darting about above the quiet surface of the water where the fish had risen.

"Darn", I thought, "they are jumping after those dragonflies!"

I knew what dragonflies were from my summers on the Cowpasture River, but I didn't have anything in my meager fly box to represent them, so I picked out the biggest, bushiest fly I had and knotted it onto my tippet.

As quietly as I could, I waded across the Firehole until I was close enough to make a cast to where I had seen the splashy rise. Glory be, I made a good cast that landed the fly about two feet above the spot where the fish had splashed. And to my surprise, a nice trout rose and slurped the big fly into its mouth. I struck and was fast to a big brown trout!

After a spirited fight, I was able to net the fish and take it to the bank. Wow, it was 18 inches at least, by far the biggest trout I had caught on a fly in Yellowstone. Now I was really hooked on fly fishing.

I quickly took my prize catch upstream to show it to the old man who was still fishing the same riffle-run where I had been watching him. He waded over to the bank to see my fish. He was very friendly and complimented me on a fine catch.

Then he did something that I didn't expect. He asked if he could see my fish, which was still alive and kicking. I handed it to him, and he quickly snapped its neck. He said, "Son, we don't want our quarry to suffer, do we?" Then he handed the fish back to me.

The old man's sentiments and what he did to my trout made a deep impression on me, and as I think back, probably was the beginning of my eventually becoming a catch-and-release fly fishing advocate.

As we walked back to the parking lot at Biscuit Basin, the old man told me that he had been fishing the waters of Yellowstone for decades and considered them to be the best trout streams in the United States. I wish I had gotten the old man's name because I have often wondered if he might not have been the angling editor of

Sports Afield, Field and Stream, or Outdoor Life, popular outdoor magazines back in the 1950s and 60s. Perhaps he was even one of my heroes, Joe Brooks, Ray Bergman or Ted Trueblood, fishing editors for those magazines who I later learned spent a great deal of time in Yellowstone. Probably not, but I like to think he might have been.

Before we parted, he used my Kodak Instamatic to snap a picture of me with my big trout beside his camper. What a memory!

*My big trout after my friend snapped its neck to keep it from suffering*

## The Madison River

The Madison River is formed by the junction of the Firehole and Gibbon rivers. In Yellowstone, the Madison is mostly a placid, smooth-flowing river, but it does have a few riffle-dominated reaches, like the Barn Holes, just inside the western border of the park and a long riffle-run alongside River Road between the west gate and Seven Mile Bridge.

During the first 25 years that I fished the Madison, I fished inside park boundaries. I generally fished upstream of Seven Mile Bridge, above the area that was restricted for the breeding of the endangered trumpeter swans. This area, along with the swifter water at the Barn Holes, was where I fished in the fall when trout were migrating up from Hebgen Lake to spawn (or, in the case of the rainbows, to eat the spawn of the browns).

*A placid stretch of the Madison River where I often fished in the fall for spawners and spawn eaters up from Hebgen Lake*

On several occasions among my many trips to Yellowstone in late September and October, I hit the spawning run just right. A favorite memory of mine is when, in 1977, I fished this reach of the river using a Heddon bamboo rod that I had just bought from an old friend in Clemson who was dying from cancer. I had always wanted to own a quality bamboo fly rod but couldn't afford one. My friend's rod was one of Heddon's best — their Model 50 Deluxe President model — and was in pristine condition. I was proud to own and fish with my "new" bamboo rod and wanted to show my friend the pictures of trout I caught on it before he passed.

This stretch of the Madison was, and probably still is, somewhat dangerous to wade due to beaver holes along the bank and frequent depressions in the river itself that are filled with deep sand and, as angling author Charlie Brooks put it, can act like quicksand. Brooks, a very experienced Yellowstone fisherman, wrote extensively about his fishing experiences in and around the park. He said he wouldn't fish this area of the Madison for any amount of money. Personally, I was glad that he wrote such an intense warning since I hoped it would keep most fishermen out of a stretch of the river that I selfishly wanted all to myself.

I was young and foolish in the 1970s and 80s, so I carefully fished this stretch using a wading stick to probe for suspicious holes. I figured the rewards were worth the risk, and they were. I caught and released a number of browns and rainbows in the 16- to 20-inch class as they made their way upstream from Hebgen Lake. I caught most of the fish on spruce fly streamers or on black and olive wooly buggers.

*Seventeen-inch brown caught on my "new" Heddon bamboo fly rod (1977) and 16-inch rainbow trout caught on my custom-made Ferdinand Claudio rod (1978) in the Madison River*

I was fortunate to have a profession that allowed me the freedom to fish and often took me to some spectacular fishing destinations. As a professor of forestry at Clemson University, I was often able to create a perfect schedule for my fly-fishing adventures. I was fortunate not to teach classes during the fall semester, using that time to present papers about my research at technical conferences. Looking back on my career, I believe the reason I immersed myself in research in such a broad range of natural resource fields — from silviculture to ecology, hydrology, forest soils, wildlife management, and even fisheries studies — was because it gave me so many opportunities to attend technical conferences and enabled me to fish all over the U.S. and Canada before or after these meetings.

Of course, it wasn't just the fishing. I enjoyed the research for its own sake as well, but the opportunity to fish certainly enhanced my desire to attend and participate in these meetings which in turn benefited my career.

As I grew older, I began to fish the Madison River outside the park more frequently. This part of the river has been described as a 50-mile riffle from Quake Lake, the epicenter of the 1959 earthquake that killed 28 people, to Ennis, Montana. Although relatively shallow, the river in this section is difficult to wade because the water is so swift and the bottom is very rocky and slippery, but it is loaded with aquatic insects, sculpins and other trout foods. It is one of the most popular trout fishing rivers in the west.

One of my fondest memories of fishing the Madison outside the park centers around the largest trout I ever caught there. In September 1986, my good friend, Rick Myers, and I took a week of annual leave from Clemson to fish the streams in and around Yellowstone.

*Netting a nice brown trout in the Madison River in 1986*

On the day I caught my big fish, we were fishing about a mile below Reynolds Bridge. Rick was downstream of me and out of sight. I was wade-fishing, slowly moving upstream, close to the bank. I approached a frothy pocket, deeper than most I had seen that morning, with a large dead cottonwood tree lying partially submerged along the shore. "There's got to be a big fish here," I thought.

Using a #4 olive girdle bug, I made a short cast into the foaming pocket. As soon as the fly hit the water, a huge brown trout charged up from below, hitting the girdle bug hard as it leaped horizontally from the water. I struck and felt the weight of the big trout before it hit the water again, but suddenly my girdle bug shot right back at me. The big fish was gone in an instant. I had just lost the biggest trout I ever hooked, or almost hooked, in Yellowstone country even though I thought I had done everything right. What a bummer!

When Rick and I met a little later on the shore for our lunch, I complained about what had happened. He was not too sympathetic, probably thinking this was just one more of the many fish tales he had heard from me — all mostly true, I might add.

"Okay, wise guy, I'll show you," I told him. "I'm going back there this afternoon and catch that fish. Be ready to eat your words." Rick loved to joke with me, and I with him.

Several hours later, I was approaching that same piece of pocket water, just as before. When I was about 30 yards from where I had previously missed the big brown, a drift boat with two anglers came into view. They were on the other side of the river, but suddenly the oarsman began rowing hard toward the middle. They got out of the boat and one of the guys held the boat beside a big rock while the other got his rod and waded to within casting distance of where "my" fish was. He began casting a big streamer fly into the frothy pocket but evidently the hex I had put on him worked. So, after about six fruitless casts he waded back to their boat, and they continued floating down the river.

I let the pocket rest for about 15 minutes, then carefully approached and made my cast. My girdle bug flew out just the right distance, but darn, the fly and tippet wrapped around a limb of that dead cottonwood. I couldn't jiggle it loose, so finally I cautiously waded up until I could free the fly with the tip of my rod. I figured that trout was not going to be caught this day.

Standing there fuming, I casually flipped the girdle bug into the next closest pocket, only about 10 feet away. Bam! I got another hard hit, and this time I had him. I'm sure it must have been the same big brown that I had just missed.

*My five-pound brown trout, caught and released below Reynolds Bridge on the Madison*

After a difficult fight, which included a dunking when I slipped off a sloping rock, soaking me and my camera, I managed to net the fish and get it to the bank to measure and take a quick picture. My wet camera provided a rather poor picture, but my Zebco De-Liar said the big male weighed five pounds and measured 23 inches, my largest trout ever in all those years of angling in Yellowstone country. After I carefully revived him in shallow water, I released my treasure back into the river.

*The Madison, where I caught my biggest Yellowstone trout*

## The Yellowstone River

My memories of the Yellowstone River go back to the early 1960s when I hiked with friends into the canyon of the Yellowstone to fish for cutthroat trout. My first time into the canyon was in late June of 1960 when a couple of friends and I hiked down the moderate to strenuous Seven Mile Hole Trail near Canyon Village that led nearly 2,000 feet down to the river. The salmon flies were hatching! Honestly, it was more like a four-mile hike than seven, but that's the trail name, and it did feel like seven miles on the hike out!

The adult stage of the two-inch long salmon flies was climbing onto stream-side bushes and rocks preparing to mate. Some would flutter clumsily in the air and fall into the water and the trout were greedily splashing after them. I picked some of the big bugs off the willows and impaled them onto my hook and readily caught a bunch of trout. Obviously, this was before I had seriously converted to a catch-and-release angler.

That experience of hiking more than four miles deep into one of the most beautiful canyons in the country, then seeing native cutthroat trout slurping up salmon flies, and then catching a string of beautiful wild trout, is one I will never forget.

Throughout the time I worked at Canyon Village in the early 1960s, I had the opportunity to fish the Yellowstone River frequently. It was only a few miles from the village to the Mud Volcano/Sulfur Caldron area of the river where an angler could wade the river and catch native cutthroat trout. The fish averaged about 15 to 17 inches.

Once while fishing in this area a huge buffalo bull suddenly appeared on the bank and stepped into the river not more than 30 yards upstream of me. Park rangers had spread the word that buffalo, not grizzly bears, were the most dangerous animal in the park, and I had gotten the message. Thankfully, that big bull had no interest in harming me and just continued across the river giving me another memory imprinted on my mind.

*A 1960 photo of my catch of cutthroat trout from the canyon of the Yellowstone River*

## The Clearwater River

I must mention one final river that played a major role in shaping my life, the Clearwater River in Idaho. For 75 miles, the Clearwater flows out of the Bitterroot Mountains on the Idaho-Montana border until it joins the Snake River at Lewiston, Idaho. The Clearwater is particularly important to me because it played a major role in drawing me to the University of Idaho where I earned a Ph.D. in forest sciences. As I was considering graduate school, I learned that the Clearwater River was 20 to 30 miles from the University of Idaho and that it had strong runs of steelhead, an anadromous version of the rainbow trout, which spends two to three years of its life at sea before migrating up rivers to spawn.

I had read all about the steelhead — about what a fabulous quarry they are for fishermen, about their great size and how hard they are to catch. I was up for the challenge, I told myself. Little did I realize how tough that challenge would be.

Despite my enthusiasm, I rarely fished for steelhead during my first year in Idaho as I was trying to make a strong positive impression on my major professor and the other committee members who would to a great extent determine the success of my Ph.D. program. But during the second and third years of my program, I made an honest effort to catch this elusive steelhead. My efforts were moderately successful. I managed to catch only 12 of them. But I loved the fight. Their size and tenacity made up for their paucity in numbers.

Eleven of my fish weighed between 12 and 17½ pounds and were caught on my new steelhead outfit — a Garcia spinning rod and a Mitchell 306 spinning reel. Eight of those fish were caught in the Clearwater River, while one was caught in each of its three major tributaries — the Lochsa, the Selway and the North Fork rivers.

The last steelhead I caught was my most memorable one. I caught it on my new 6-weight Fenwick fiberglass fly rod using a green-butt skunk fly that I tied myself. The steelhead weighed nine pounds, my smallest, but it proved to me that I could hook and land large powerful fish on a fly rod, a lesson that has stood the test of time for me.

*My nine-pound steelhead, caught on a green-butt skunk fly*

There were very few fly fishermen fishing for steelhead in Idaho in the mid-1960s when I caught mine. I got the urge to try my hand at it after reading an article in the Spokane Chronicle by an outdoor writer named Fenton Roskelley telling readers exactly how to catch a steelhead on a fly in the Clearwater River. He thoroughly described using a technique that included fishing three- to four-foot-deep riffles as they slowed into a pool, with ever lengthening casts of a weighted green-butt skunk fly, swung across and down the current. On my third or fourth attempt, I finally hooked and landed my first and only steelhead on a fly, the nine-pounder!

The Clearwater River drew me to the University of Idaho and on to a Ph.D. in forest sciences. That experience led me to the University of Florida for a post-doctorate position, then to Kentucky as a research forester with the U.S. Forest Service and finally to Clemson University where I became a chaired professor in the Forest Resources Department for 35 years. Without question, I would say that the Clearwater River played an important and obvious role in helping to shape my life.

But I would argue that all these rivers shaped the direction of my life and helped me determine a path. Once I started on that path, they continued to bring pleasure and comfort to me throughout my life. Now an old man, I am thankful for the rivers that led me to this point in my life. Without the joy and peace that fishing in these rivers gave me, I can't imagine how different my life would have been.

# Fishing: My Life-Long Addiction
*David Van Lear*

Psychiatrists consider addiction to be a brain disease causing individuals to be compulsive users of harmful substances despite the often-disastrous consequences. In fact, when medical professionals talk about addictions, they are normally talking about substance abuse such as illegal drugs, alcohol, or cigarettes. However, I believe certain activities can be "addictive" but without the harmful effects of ingesting substances like drugs and alcohol. The type of addiction I am referring to produces mental and physical benefits that may last a lifetime.

My addiction is to fishing. While most fishermen would not say they are addicted to fishing, a few might admit it. Happily, I am one of those. I became addicted to fishing at a very young age.

The stage for my addiction was set in the summer of 1952 on the Cowpasture River near Clifton Forge, Virginia, when I experienced the thrill of successfully landing my first real catch – a large smallmouth bass. Even though I made novice mistakes and thought much of that catch was beginner's luck, I had caught a three-pound smallmouth bass, a very nice bass for the Cowpasture River, and the early seeds of my addiction to fishing had been sown.

As I progressed through my teenage years, I grew to love fishing more and more. My dad, through contacts at his small grocery store, had permission from several landowners to fish beautiful stretches of the river. In the summers and falls throughout my high school years, Dad and I would fish together about once a week, usually on Wednesday afternoons when he closed his store. Occasionally — very occasionally — we caught a nice bass in the three- to four- pound class.

*The Cowpasture River where my addiction began*

When we would catch a big one, we would give each other a big hug, which strengthened the bond between us and further fueled the addiction I was developing for fishing. I simply loved to fish.

When I graduated from high school in 1958, my best friend and I went to Yellowstone National Park for summer jobs cleaning the tourist cabins at Old Faithful. My brother, who had worked in the park the previous summer, had told us about the wonderful trout fishing there and encouraged us to go. My friend Richard and I had fished for trout in the small creeks around our hometown of Clifton Forge but had never experienced trout fishing like we would find in Yellowstone. There, my addiction to fishing grew even stronger.

*A brown trout from Iron Creek in Yellowstone National Park in 1958*

Richard and I lived in barracks for park employees that were only a 15-minute hike to a beautiful little stream called Iron Creek that was loaded with trout and where we could use our spinning outfits. We seemed to be the only ones that fished the creek, and we caught lots of trout, including our biggest of the summer — a four-pound brown trout that Richard caught. Iron Creek was all that we could have hoped for, a tranquil meadow stream full of wild trout that felt like it was all ours.

Happily, my growing fishing addiction seemed to have only positive effects on my mental and physical health, which in turn reinforced the addiction.

I would return to Yellowstone for four more summers while I pursued my B.S. and M.S. in forestry at Virginia Tech. During these summers, I gradually switched my method of fishing from spin fishing to fly fishing, and the addiction only grew stronger. I loved everything about fly fishing, from the longer rods to the relatively tiny flies on the end of my leader, to the gorgeous environments of most trout streams and the remarkable beauty of the trout themselves. I also began to engulf myself in the rich literature of fly fishing.

My third summer in Yellowstone was my trout-fishing peak. By then, I had a car enabling me to fish Yellowstone's world-famous trout streams, like the Madison, Firehole, Gibbon, Gallatin and others. And I did fish, often alone because none of my friends, some of whom had come back to the park multiple years like I did, had the fishing fever like me.

When I decided to continue my education and work toward a Ph.D., I selected the University of Idaho because it had a solid reputation as a good forestry school, was located in the Rocky Mountains which I had grown to love, and was close to the Clearwater River, which had runs of steelhead, an ocean-going rainbow trout that could weigh up to 20 pounds or more. My dilemma was whether I would have time to work on a Ph.D. in forest sciences — no easy task — and fish for steelhead, too. My addicted mind told me I could do it.

During my three years at the university, I managed to catch only a dozen steelhead, the hardest fish that I had ever tried to catch. I once fished twelve times in a row without a strike from one of these migrating giants, wading in the icy Clearwater River, fingers numb, with ice in the guides on my rod. "Only a fool would fish like this," I thought, but my addiction kept me going. Finally, when I felt the strike of one of those giant trout (my largest was 17½ pounds) the wait was well worth it. Steelheads would explode down the river, going back toward the Pacific from whence they came, usually jumping a couple of times on their first downstream run, then fighting doggedly for the next few minutes as they tried to escape. Once they were hooked, I was generally able to land them.

All but one of those dozen steelhead I caught were on spinning gear, and that one exception was special. I caught her on my new Fenwick fly rod using a green-butt skunk fly pattern that I tied myself. It was the smallest of the twelve steelhead I caught, weighing 9 pounds, but it proved to me that I could hook and land large, strong and explosive fish on a fly rod, a lesson I wouldn't soon forget.

Steelhead clearly fueled my addiction.

After receiving my doctorate, the lure of fishing and a chance to work in the southeastern United States drew me to the University of Florida for a postdoctoral position in a forest nutrition project aimed at increasing growth of pine stands on private industrial lands. The job fit nicely with one of my long-time fishing goals —

catching a 10-pound largemouth bass. I thought Florida would be my best chance.

During my year in Florida, fishing with my friend Joel Smith, I caught five bass that we thought would have weighed 10 pounds if they had not been caught immediately after spawning. Instead, they weighed only about 8½ pounds each. So, I still didn't have my 10-pounder. But I still had my addiction!

*My largest steelhead (17½ pounds) and my favorite (a nine-pounder) caught on a fly*

When my postdoctoral appointment ended, I accepted a position with the U.S. Forest Service in Kentucky still hoping for my dream bass. During some time off from work, I returned to Florida to try my luck again at catching that elusive 10-pound largemouth. This time, it was mid-February, before the spawn.

Joel's work responsibilities kept him from fishing with me that first day, so I told him sarcastically, "I'm really sorry about that, Joel, I really am, but I'm going to have to fish anyway. I'll catch a big one for you." So, I found my way through the longleaf pine-scrub oak forest near Gainesville to a small pond that Joel had shown me the previous year.

As I waded out into the pond, I saw the swept-out bed of a spawning bass, clearly visible where the white sand was exposed after the dark organic muck was swept away by smaller male bass. While I watched the bed, a large dark shadow swam over it. My God, that was a big bass! I quickly took a large bullhead minnow from my bait bucket, hooked it through the lips, and cast it about five feet beyond the bed. Then I slowly pulled the minnow back until I thought it was sitting on the bed. I waited.

After a few minutes, my line jerked and started to move away, being pulled hard and steady. I let the fish run and run some more. When it stopped, I leaned forward, reeled in the slack line, and struck hard. Nothing was there, but off to my left a big fish rolled on the surface. Was that my fish? I was sure it was. The fish had eaten my minnow and run straight away from me, passing some rushes sticking out of the water, and taking a hard left. While I knew I had not gotten a solid strike on her, I had not realized her sudden change of direction when I first struck. I had her direction now, so I quickly reeled up more slack and struck again.

This time she was hooked solidly. She wallowed to the surface again, and headed toward an old, barbed wire fence that stretched across the upper end of the pond. If she got tangled in that, I would lose her for sure.

Fortunately, I was able to stop her before she got to the fence. After a few more wallows on the surface — she was probably too heavy to jump clear of the water — I was able to grab her by the lower jaw and haul her to the bank. I could tell by her heft that this might be my elusive 10-pound bass and, sure enough, my Zebco de-liar said 10½ pounds! Back at Joel's lab, she weighed two ounces less than that, but still I could cross the 10-pound bass off my bucket list.

*My 10-pound bass from a north-Florida pond*

My professional career took me to Clemson in 1971 as an associate professor in the forestry department. Fortunately for my addiction, I did not teach in the fall semester. This meant I could often schedule fishing excursions to the Rockies or other locations when I attended professional meetings to present papers about my research. If the meetings were west of the Mississippi River, I figured that was close enough to the Rockies for me to take a few days of annual leave, rent a car and get in some trout fishing. No need to even try to beat this healthy fishing addiction.

Fishing was a habit that made me feel better both mentally and physically. A day or two spent fishing in a gorgeous environment, like wading a gin-clear trout stream in the Rockies or the southern Appalachians and casting a fly to rising trout or fishing for bass on a quiet evening with a good friend, certainly helped clear my mind of the distractions and pressures of work. It also made me better able to concentrate on my teaching and research duties, making me more effective and productive in these endeavors.

*Fighting a cutthroat trout on a Wyoming stream*

The joy of fishing wasn't confined just to catching big fish; catching small fish was almost as enjoyable, if not quite as memorable. And I didn't have to go long distances to get my fishing "fix." I frequently fished trout streams and bass lakes in North and South Carolina, Georgia and Tennessee, all within a few hours away from my home base.

While I have been a practitioner of "catch and release" for about 60 years, I kept some of my trophies and had them mounted, like my 10-pound brown trout and my 10-pound largemouth bass. I occasionally kept a few fish to eat. But generally, I returned my catches to their homes. I thought nothing could be better for a fisherman and the sport than to catch a trout or a bass on a fly or bass bug he had tied himself, and then release that fish to fight again another day.

*My 10-pound brown trout from Lake Jocassee in 1984*

Over the decades, fishing pressure on our streams and lakes has increased and the best way to help sustain a quality fishery was to release the catch so those fish could grow larger and be available for other anglers to catch. In my mind, the sport of fishing couldn't get much better than that.

There are some exceptions to the catch-and-release rule. Some streams become too warm as the season progresses and the mortality of released fish would be unacceptably high.

Of course, there is nothing wrong with keeping a fish or a stringer of fish if you plan to eat them. I did that for a long time as a young fisherman. But as I matured as an angler, it gave me greater enjoyment to release the fish I had fairly caught to help ensure the sustainability of the resource, something a fisherman who is also a forester always has on his mind.

*Fly fishing a trout stream in the mountains of South Carolina*

During the 35 years that I taught at Clemson, my wife Carolyn and I made many trips to the northern Rockies, often to Yellowstone, to play tourist and satisfy my fishing addiction. During those trips, Carolyn would stay in the little town of West Yellowstone and shop or browse, while I would drive into the park and fish one of its famous trout streams. In the afternoon, we would tour the park together for a few hours, sometimes driving south to the Grand Tetons National Park, where I occasionally fished the Snake, Gros Ventre, and Hoback rivers, and Flat Creek. On a few occasions, we would drive north, about 400 miles, to Glacier National Park and then on to Alberta or British Columbia where I fished the Bow and Elk rivers.

*Guide Mike Guinn nets my 20-inch rainbow from the Bow River in Alberta, Canada, in 1996*

After fishing for almost seven decades, I think I've earned the right to use the word "addiction." I also think this addiction has gone beyond satisfying my need to fish to help me maintain balance, keeping my moods on an even keel.

In the last decade, I've fished much less frequently. At 82 years of age and with some health issues, I've experienced some balance problems. For a fisherman, that means I have fallen in — really fallen in, like total immersion from head to toe — three out of the last four times I have been trout fishing on the Chattooga and Chauga rivers in South Carolina I took a soaking. Luckily, I fell in water a few feet deep and not on rocks that were everywhere around me. I lost my dignity but avoided a broken hip, the last thing I need at this stage of my life.

Although I'm not wade fishing mountain trout streams that much anymore, I still go on guided float trips occasionally, like down the Chattahoochee River below Lake Lanier in Georgia. I also enjoy fishing small ponds around Clemson for bass and bluegills where the threat of bodily harm in case of a slip or misstep is not too great.

But I am still an addict. I simply can't let it go. These days, instead of being out on the stream, I choose mostly to write about fishing, as I did in two books, Memories Made and Lessons Learned During a Lifetime of Angling and Turning Points in the Life of a Fisherman, written when I was 70 and 80 years old, respectively. I add to those books a gathering of this and other short stories. Although not the same as fishing, writing about experiences on the water is almost as good as fishing when you enjoy it as much as I do. Taken all together, the fishing, the friends and the writing have improved my mental and physical health, helping me have a successful and happy life.

# A GRIZZLY ENCOUNTER

I began my love affair with Yellowstone National Park when I was 17 years old. Over the years, I would go back to that wonderful park many, many times, but that first year, I went with my friend and fishing buddy, Richard, to work in the park — and to fish, of course. Richard and I had just graduated from high school, and we were ready for adventure.

That summer, Richard and I worked as cabin boys, cleaning the camper cabins at Old Faithful Lodge. After cleaning our allotted cabins, which we usually accomplished by about three in the afternoon, we would grab our fishing rods and walk about a mile through the woods behind our barracks to a beautiful meadow stream called Iron Creek. It was loaded with wild brown and rainbow trout and, in its upper reaches, even had some eastern brook trout. Richard and I fished this stream about two or three times each week.

I was in fly-fisherman's heaven. And, while Richard could not go back to the park after that first summer, I continued to work in Yellowstone for four more summers — one summer at Old Faithful Lodge and three more at Canyon Village, each time as a bellhop. I still fished Iron Creek occasionally, even when I worked at Canyon Lodge, sometimes alone, sometimes with a buddy or two. And sometimes with uninvited companions.

Even after fishing Iron Creek many times, I was always a little apprehensive when I fished there, especially when I was fishing alone. I knew that there had been a number of grizzly-bear encounters with fishermen that summer on the nearby Firehole River. So far, none had resulted in mauling or deaths.

The area was a fly-fishing mecca. Iron Creek flows into the Firehole, one of the most famous trout streams in the park, just a few hundred yards upstream from Biscuit Geyser Basin. Because of my uneasiness when fishing alone in bear country, I made a habit of keeping up a rather loud conservation with my imaginary fishing buddy, "Fred," hoping that any bears that might be in the neighborhood would assume that I wasn't alone.

Late in the summer of 1961, two of my bellhop friends and I drove to Iron Creek from Canyon Village for an afternoon of fishing. We parked in the parking lot for Black Sand Basin, a geyser basin about two miles upstream from Biscuit Basin and began to rig up. My buddies were using spinning rods, so they had their gear ready to go before I could thread my line through all the guides on my fly rod. By the time I was rigged up, my buddies had already started fishing downstream from the geyser basin. I didn't want to fish behind them because I thought that they would have spooked the trout, making them more difficult to catch, so I walked upstream of the basin and began fishing.

I had fished upstream for about a half mile, catching a few small trout, when I began to feel a little anxious about my situation. I knew there had been grizzlies in the area, and I was all alone (not counting "Fred"). My buddies by now were probably a mile below Black Sand Basin — out of sight and hearing range. Additionally, while there had been a few tourists walking the boardwalk at Morning Glory Pool, one of the most famous hot springs in the park, when I had started fishing upstream hours earlier, I was far away from that spot now.

The forest and grassy meadow along Iron Creek, still soggy and ripe with mosquitos this early in the summer, suddenly seemed unnaturally quiet to me. Still talking rather loudly to "Fred," I climbed out of the stream and crept along the more timbered west bank, sneaking up on the next fishy-looking run. All at once, I began to feel like I wasn't alone on the stream — it was just too quiet.

The cause of my feeling soon became apparent.

As I rounded a bend in the stream, there — no more than 30 yards ahead — stood a mother grizzly and her two half-grown cubs. They were looking right at me. To make matters worse, the grizzlies were on the same side of the creek as me, all of them just staring at me. They were so close that I could have cast my fly to them. I knew that with just a few bounds, they could be on me, and I would be their lunch.

There was no doubt in my mind that these were grizzly bears, not black bears. I was very familiar with black bears, having helped chase dozens of them away from their raids on garbage cans when

I was a cabin boy at Old Faithful Lodge. No. These were definitely grizzlies: concave faces, pronounced hump on their backs and grizzled brown fur. They had all the distinctive characteristics of grizzlies. And grizzlies, I knew, were a much more formidable bear than the black bear.

My mind raced. What should I do? The bears could be on me in seconds and maul me to pieces. I knew I couldn't outrun them since grizzlies can outrun the fastest human sprinters. And I did not want to trigger a predator-prey response in those bears, especially not with me being the prey!

The grizzlies kept their eyes on me as I started slowly backing away. For some reason, I began making a low moaning sound, thinking (I don't know why) that the sound might make the bears sense I wasn't afraid. And I wasn't afraid. Hell, I was terrified! My heart felt like it would thump out of my chest.

As I was slowly backing away, I stumbled and fell over a dead lodgepole pine tree, one of millions such trees lying on the ground in the park. I dropped my fly rod and my pipe fell out of my mouth. As I got to my feet, the mother bear jerked her head to the left, and the cubs immediately turned and ran back behind her into the dense woods.

Now it was just mama bear and me staring at each other from a distance of about 35 yards. Glancing behind me, I saw two pine trees, about six to eight inches in diameter, growing about three feet apart. They were just a short distance away, so I moved very slowly toward them, keeping a wary eye on the bear. When I reached the trees, I stepped between them and, with the help of a major adrenaline rush, spread-eagled my way up to the lowest live branches which were about 12 to 15 feet above the ground. Then I scooted over to the largest of the two trees and climbed farther up, stopping only when I was about 20 feet off the ground.

*View of Iron Creek from 20 feet up a lodgepole pine tree*

I was feeling a little safer. I knew that adult grizzlies did not climb trees — at least that's what I had read in outdoor magazines back in the early 1960s. However, I certainly didn't like the idea of being the guy to test that theory. Additionally, while I had been climbing up the two trees, the mother grizzly had started walking slowly toward me. She stopped within 10 feet of my tree, and I remember looking down on her; the brownish-silver hair on her back was standing straight up — like a mad dog's, I thought. Her eyes were as black as obsidian.

*An over-dramatized wood carving I made of me climbing a tree to escape a charging grizzly*

She stood there for a few seconds, looking up at me, and then turned and headed back into the woods where the cubs had run. I was in no hurry to leave the tree, and about 10 minutes later, while I was still up there, she came back to the spot where I had originally seen her and the cubs. She didn't seem to want to leave that spot. I didn't know why, but I later speculated that I might have interrupted their meal. They may have been eating an elk calf that they had killed. Perhaps that's why they didn't run into the woods when "Fred" and I approached, "conversing" loudly with each other. Normally, unless they were guarding food, bears will move away when they hear people approaching.

Finally, the grizzly left. But just to be safe, I stayed up that pine tree for about 45 minutes before, not seeing any sign of her, I climbed down to the lowest dead limb, hung from it and dropped to the ground. I snatched up my fishing rod, wasted no time looking for my pipe, hopped across Iron Creek in two or three bounds, ran until out of breath and then walked rapidly across the long grassy meadow back to Black Sand Basin. I was safe at last, and with a memory that I was sure would last a lifetime. And it has.

*In later years, I came to believe that the mother grizzly and her two cubs were killed that same summer by park rangers. There were numerous bear-fishermen incidents reported in 1961 near the Firehole River that escalated as the summer progressed until it became necessary for the Park Service to remove the bears.*

*Two summers later, in 1963, the last summer I worked in the park, I visited the Canyon Village Visitor Center. There, I saw a mounted mother grizzly and two cubs that looked eerily similar to the bears I had encountered on Iron Creek. Years later, in 2008, my wife Carolyn and I visited the Yellowstone Fishing Bridge Visitor Center where the same bears were then being displayed. There, a Park Ranger told me that they were killed in 1961, the same year I was treed. I would bet they were "my" bears.*

# TURN AROUND!

As I approached Montrose, Colorado, a highway sign pointed the way to the Black Canyon of the Gunnison River. I was driving from Virginia to Yellowstone National Park for another fly-fishing "fix." I had fallen in love with Yellowstone National Park when I had worked there during five summers after high school graduation. There is where I learned to fly fish and established a life-long addiction.

Naturally, given the opportunity in 1971, I headed back to Yellowstone. I had chosen a southern route so I could see and perhaps fish a couple of the beautiful streams in Colorado before reaching Yellowstone. I only had about 10 days before I would report to my new job at Clemson University, so time was short. When I reached Durango, Colorado, in the southwest corner of the state, I headed north on Route 550 toward Montrose.

The Black Canyon of the Gunnison River sounded like a place worth seeing. Maybe, I thought, I could fish the river for half a day or so. The right turn I took outside of Montrose, Colorado, proved to be a real turning point — one of many— that helped determine the direction of my life.

That particular turn also almost cost me my life.

**There must be a way down.**

The Black Canyon of the Gunnison would be made a national park in 1999, but that was still 28 years in the future. The canyon was awesome — more impressive in some ways than the Grand Canyon of the Yellowstone River, a canyon I was intimately familiar with from my summers spent working in the park. Several times I had hiked with friends into the Yellowstone canyon to fish for cutthroat trout during the salmonfly hatch, and not once did I feel in danger of falling. I had to be careful, yes, but I had not been in imminent danger.

On this Sunday morning as I drove along the south rim, the Black Canyon of the Gunnison had a different feel from the bright and beautiful canyon of the Yellowstone that I was so familiar with. This canyon felt deeper, darker and narrower. It seemed more dangerous and foreboding, and most important of all, there did not appear to be any reasonable way to access the river I saw far below.

As I walked along the rim of the canyon, I noticed a small sign that read "Good Trout Fishing 2,000 Feet Below." It didn't say anything about how to get down there, and I didn't see any trails leading to the river. How could I access the river?

Since no one was around on that quiet, rather lonely, morning who could answer that question for me, I started looking around for myself. Surely one of the many ravines, or washes, that fell sharply off the rim would lead an angler down to the river. Why would there be a sign advertising the trout fishing down in the canyon if there was no way to get down there?

Several of the ravines appeared to lead at least halfway down to the river, but from the rim it was impossible to see beyond those inflection points. Being a young bachelor at the time, without anyone to reprimand me for being so stupid, I decided to give the most promising of those ravines a try. I put on my waders, laced on my hiking boots, grabbed my fly rod and fishing vest, and started climbing and sliding on my rear end down the ravine.

What a brainless decision that was! After I had climbed and slid about halfway down to the river, the ravine suddenly gave way to an almost-vertical drop of at least 1,000 feet. I was just one step from eternity!

*The Black Canyon of the Gunnison, a canyon where I climbed and slid halfway to the river below before being forced to turn back by a 1,000-foot vertical drop.*

"Good grief!" I yelled (or something like that), as I struggled to stabilize my position to avoid sliding over the brink. Catching my breath, I realized what a foolish idea this had been. If I had gone another foot, I would have slid off into nothing and fallen to my death.

No one would have known where I was. I hadn't told anyone of my stupid idea to access the Gunnison River by climbing down into the canyon. In my mind, I pictured a fisherman or floater one day discovering a scavenger-ravaged body and wondered how it got there. "Surely not from above," they would think. "Only a fool would attempt to climb down that cliff!"

Gathering my wits, I carefully reversed direction and slowly, on hands and knees, crawled up and out of the ravine. As far as I know, no one saw this brilliant show of stupidity.

A life of addiction

I readily admit an addiction to fly fishing. And sometimes I have wondered if this addiction is so deeply ingrained in my being that I cannot make rational decisions. Looking back on the Black Canyon experience, I know I learned a lesson, but it could have been my final lesson. What a dangerous risk I took just to fly fish that river!

In other aspects of my life, I think I make fairly normal decisions, including some great decisions, like marrying my wife Carolyn, but with fly fishing, I have often wondered how sound my decisions were.

That Sunday morning, I was able to get back in my truck and travel on to Yellowstone, where grizzly bears were the only things I had to worry about.

# FISHING ADVENTURES WITH DOC AND WILLY

In 1971, I arrived at Clemson University to begin a career as a professor of forestry. I was a young bachelor and soon realized that I needed a good dog for company. Lucky indeed, I was offered a little pup by some friends who raised basset hounds. I named my new dog Doc.

Doc was a registered basset hound, just six months old with beautiful brown, black and white markings, sad eyes, long ears, and a lame right front leg, which sometimes made him trip himself when he stepped on one of his ears.

Doc liked to go fishing with my good friend, Willy Williams, and me in my small bass boat. He often would sit in the bottom of the boat, prop his front legs on the bow and let his long ears flap in the breeze as we motored around Lake Hartwell, a 50,000-acre lake adjacent to the Clemson University campus. It was quite a sight!

There were many memorable happenings when Doc was in the boat with us, but two were particularly special.

The first incident occurred one day when Doc was sitting on the bow of the boat. He liked to do this when we were just using the trolling motor and not going too fast. So, on this spring day he was sitting on the bow when the boat suddenly hit a submerged stump. With a splash, Doc went head-first into the lake.

*My basset pup, Doc*

With their thick, heavy bodies and short legs, basset hounds are definitely not designed for swimming. Doc barely floated when he hit the water. He was sinking fast when I was able to grab him by his collar and pull him back into the boat. I believe he would have drowned if I hadn't been able to grab him.

Needless to say, that experience cured Doc's urge to sit on the bow of the boat.

The second "Doc incident" was even more serious for Doc and for me. One day while fishing, I was changing lures, and had just picked a Rapala from my tackle box. The Rapala is a minnow-shaped lure with treble hooks on each end. Curious as to what I was doing, Doc came over to investigate. Unfortunately, as he sniffed around, one of the hooks caught him in the nose. As he jerked away in pain, another of the treble hooks caught me in the thumb. We were caught together!

Doc didn't like this situation one bit, and I didn't care much for it either! He began walking toward the back of the boat, trying to shake that darn thing from his nose. I was in close pursuit trying to mimic his every move with my hand and his nose attached by sharp hooks to the same lure.

"Willy, help me!" I yelled. "Get on Doc's back and hold his head still so I can get myself unhooked from this darn lure."

Willy quickly came to the rescue. I don't know what I would have done if Willy hadn't jumped on Doc's back and grabbed his head in a vice-like grip. Thankfully, the hook in my thumb had not penetrated beyond the barb so I was able to free myself rather easily. But there was no such luck for poor ol' Doc. The hook in his nose had entered through his nostril and couldn't be backed out. It was embedded beyond the barb.

"Willy, we're gonna have to push the hook all the way through his nose so we can clip off the barb and back the hook out." Sounds simple, but a hound dog's nose is about as tough as football leather. Still, if we could push the hook through, we could clip off the barb with our fishing pliers. Then we would be able to back the hook out. That was the plan.

Doc was such a brave warrior as we pushed the hook through to the outside of his nose. And, after clipping off the barb, Doc and

I were finally free of those dastardly hooks! Doc seemed to tell us, "You can keep your darned old Rapala. I didn't want it anyway!" He rested on the bottom of the boat for a few minutes before he got to his feet, and playfully lunged at Willy, as if trying to push him into the lake for jumping on his back during his painful ordeal.

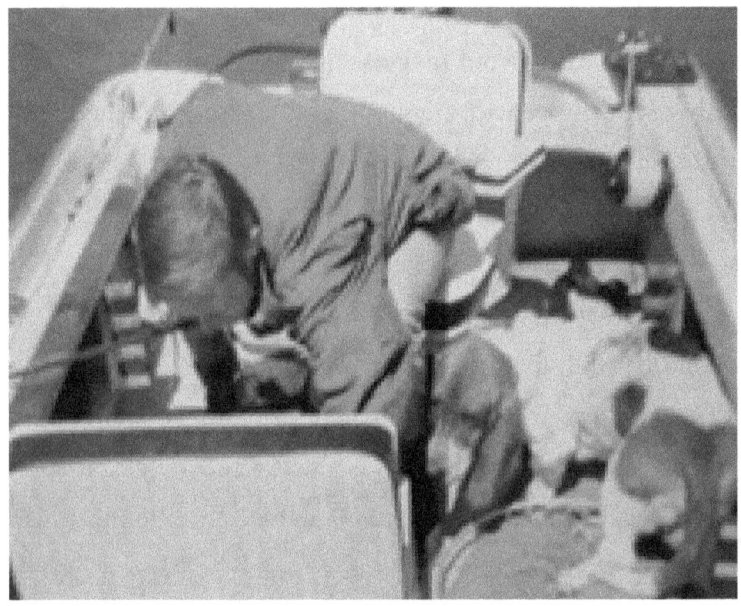

*Willy and Doc minutes before the treble hook incident*

However, within minutes, Doc was his old, sweet self, another wonderful characteristic of dogs. Generally, if you are sweet to them, they don't hold grudges.

Doc and Willy fished with me for at least 10 years, fishing for bass and hybrids, in Lake Hartwell and other regional lakes.

Together, they gave me treasured memories of fishing and friendship that I will never forget.

# SEMI-INVALID TO ACTIVE OLD MAN
*(HOW EXERCISE CHANGED MY LIFE)*

In 2005, the year I retired from Clemson University, I learned I had diabetes. I wasn't too concerned with the diagnosis and continued with my unhealthy lifestyle — eating desserts and not exercising as I should. It wasn't until I almost lost my life in an automobile accident that I became serious about treating my diabetes and improving my health.

I had driven to Atlanta to fish the Chattahoochee River with one of my former graduate students, Kyle Burrell. I have been an avid fisherman all my life and jumped at the opportunity to fish the Chattahoochee with Kyle, an expert fly fisherman who guides professionally on the river during the winter months.

I left early in the morning — about 5 a.m. — to make the two-hour drive to meet Kyle at an angler access point on the outskirts of Atlanta. We fished all morning and I had very good luck, catching 36 trout by Kyle's count — no big ones but lots of action. When I left Kyle to drive back home, I noticed that I was feeling very tired. I had not yet learned that major fluctuations in your blood sugar can cause extreme tiredness, but I was soon to find out.

As I drove northeast out of Atlanta on Interstate 85, I began to feel like dozing off. Rather than pulling off the road to rest, I continued driving, thinking I could make it home, which was only about an hour away. I was in the left lane driving about 70 mph when I felt a sudden loud jar on the passenger side of my pickup.

I had fallen asleep and drifted into the trailer of a big semi, hitting it just in front of the back wheels! The loud noise I heard was the sound of my pickup truck's passenger side mirror being folded back against the door.

The mirror had collided with the steel band at the bottom of the trailer. Only the height of my pickup kept me from going under the trailer and being crushed by the rear wheels. If I had driven down in my Camry, which I almost did that morning, I would have drifted under the trailer and been killed for sure.

That experience was more than enough incentive for me to take my diabetes seriously. Sure, I still ate sweets, but in moderation, and I began to exercise frequently. Exercising, including walking, and medication have done wonders for my blood sugar. But diabetes was just the beginning of my health's downward spiral that began in my early 70s.

About 10 years ago, I began having some minor pains in my lower abdomen. I didn't think much about it, although the thought of kidney stones crossed my mind. I had had about a dozen kidney stones in my adult life, starting when I was in my early thirties and continuing until I was about 65. Some stones I passed rather easily, while others caused excruciating pain that sent me to the emergency room.

One of the worst attacks happened on a flight to California to attend a meeting. That was a bad attack and the pain caused me to break into a cold sweat somewhere between Chicago and Pasadena. When we finally landed, I was rushed to a hospital.

After a couple days without passing the stone, the hospital urologist recommended lithotripsy, a procedure where a patient is placed horizontally in a tub of warm water and the stone is bombarded with ultrasound shock waves until it is busted into smaller particles that can be passed naturally. My sweet wife flew out to California to be with me during this ordeal and my shattered kidney stone passed a day later.

But this time the sharp pains in my abdomen did not feel like the kidney stones I had grown accustomed to. An ultrasound scan in my doctor's office indicated something much worse, so she sent me to a surgeon who confirmed her suspicions. The next week the surgeon operated and removed my cancerous left kidney. The operation was a remarkable success, and I have had no recurrence of that cancer in over 10 years.

As I recovered from cancer surgery, pain in my back began showing its ugly face. As the pain got worse, I would bend over to relieve some of the pain, but this poor posture increased my risk of falling. And fall I did, several times, along with many near falls and stumbles. Fortunately, I was never seriously injured by these falls, but they made me afraid to walk without a cane or walking stick. I eventually bought a motorized scooter that took me where I needed to go.

Finally, the pain in my back got so bad that I was referred to another surgeon who diagnosed my stumbling and falling problems as being caused by normal pressure hydrocephalus, i.e., excess water or spinal fluid on the brain. She recommended surgery to place a shunt from the ventricles in my brain down into my abdomen where the excess fluid could be absorbed.

*Dolly and me on my scooter four years ago*

The shunt did remove excess fluid but, darn, it wasn't long before I was bent over and stumbling again from persistent pain in my back. This time another surgeon said I would need surgery to remove a spur from my spine. So, about two years after my brain surgery I went back into the operating room. This operation relieved my pain for a short time, but pain and discomfort soon reappeared.

Now doctors said my pain was due to inflamed arthritis and a slipped disc, and I would need more surgery to correct the problem. Damnation, I thought. I've already had three serious surgeries in about six years, and now I was facing another. But what was I to do? I was still having back pain, still using a motorized scooter and cane to get around, and generally being a couch potato — essentially living the life of a semi-invalid. My health was in a downward spiral, but could I do anything about it?

I was about 77 years old when a lightbulb finally came on, and I realized that I needed to change my lifestyle. My epiphany came four years ago when our activities director took a group of Clemson Down's residents to tour the Biltmore House in Asheville, North Carolina. At the time, I was unable to walk very far, even with my walker, and, embarrassingly, I had to ask Nikki, our activities director, to roll me around the grounds, which she willingly did. That's when it hit me right between the eyes — I had to make some changes or my health was going to continue to decline. I wasn't ready for that.

Depressed and not wanting another surgery, I consulted my brain surgeon for a second opinion about another back operation. She reviewed my X-rays and MRIs and sent me to a pain-management clinic in Anderson, rather than recommending more surgery.

Her recommendation was the first step in my recovery from being a semi-invalid to becoming a healthy old man.

The pain management specialist determined that I was suffering from inflamed arthritis in my lower spine. Rather than surgery, he injected steroids in the area, a slightly painful procedure but not too bad, even for a wimp like me. Within days the pain was gone, and now I could stand upright.

But how would I begin to revamp my life from being a couch potato to being active enough to do the things I wanted to do? The first thing I had to do was change my mental outlook on life. I needed to start thinking positively and learning how to walk again. And, I had to learn how to exercise and lose the weight I had gained while sitting on my butt for years.

I had lots of incentives to get my health back. First, it would make me happy, a feeling we all want, and I would be able to enjoy visits with my wife, who was in Health Care at Clemson Downs. And finally, I would be able to do activities like hiking and fishing that I had always enjoyed before all these health problems.

So, how did I do it? The first thing was to learn to walk again. It had been years since I walked freely without a cane. I had almost forgotten how. I began by taking small steps and walking short distances, concentrating intently on my balance and destination. I practiced this seemingly simple activity until I felt confident in walking farther and farther without a cane. After a couple of weeks, I was able to walk over to Health Care and visit with Carolyn, which made me feel good and want to do more.

Then my wonderful caregiver, Diane, insisted I go to the daily exercise program here at the Downs. At first, I resisted, but Diane is a very forceful woman who doesn't easily take no for an answer, so I grudgingly gave in. And it was one of the best things I have ever done for myself, and it could be the same for others!

The exercise leaders in my class teach a seated exercise program that lasts about 45 minutes each weekday and works every joint in your body, from neck to ankles. Calling it a "seated exercise program" might make you think it is easy, but believe me, it is plenty strenuous for us old timers. We do seated aerobics, weight training, flexibility exercises and other exercises to increase our endurance, balance, strength and mobility. Everyone can proceed at their own pace, so you don't need to be intimidated by those who have been exercising for a longer time.

The program incorporates a walking component where a small group walks five times a week for about 30 to 45 minutes around the campus, with occasional trips to the Clemson University Experimental Forest and the South Carolina Botanical Garden.

To put it simply, exercise and walking changed my life. I went from being a semi-invalid to being a healthy old man. And it was fun along the journey.

Thanks to the exercise and walking program here at the Downs, I have made remarkable progress. Some people tell me I am a walking miracle, but I wouldn't call it a miracle — rather it was more of what my caregiver calls a change of my attitude from "I can't" to "I think I can." And it took determination to get up and get going.

It worked. I now walk several times a day, striving to get 8,000 to 10,000 steps in every day, and I have little fear of falling. My mind seems clearer, my muscle tone is much better, and I have more energy. As a side benefit, I have lost 20 pounds and about two inches off my waist! And I can go trout fishing again.

I am not writing this to brag about my progress. (I generally save my bragging for my fish stories.) I'm writing to encourage, even inspire, residents at the Downs and other retirement centers to turn their lives around and get involved in the physical activities that are offered. I truly believe that if I can do it, you can, too. These activities can change your life for the better, like it did mine. My exercise class has people from age 90 to 100 and they are amazing, living proof of what an active lifestyle can do for you.

*Trout fishing on the Chauga, again!*

## YOU CAN GO HOME AGAIN

*(At Least I Did)*

Thomas Wolfe, the famous 20th-century author, entitled one of his novels "You Can't Go Home Again." He meant, I believe, that anyone who goes back home after an absence will find everything has changed — home just won't be the same. Although I had never thought too much about that idea, I guess I had always believed it to be true. Recently, however, I discovered that Wolfe's premise may not always hold true and that, in fact, I could go home again.

In September 2019, two of my former graduate students, Rick Myers and Jud Alden, invited me to go to Virginia and fish the Calfpasture River over the Columbus Day weekend. I initially declined because I was concerned that my wife Carolyn, who was in health care at Clemson Downs, the retirement center where we lived, would worry too much about me. But then our caregiver, a wonderful woman named Diane Blackmon, who had helped my wife and me for seven years at the time, forcefully told me that I was going on this fishing trip. She would take care of Carolyn and our little dog,

Dolly. She said I had worked too hard over the past year to improve my physical condition not to go. She thought I could withstand the rigors of walking and wading the rocky shoreline of a small Virginia river for six to seven hours. This may sound like a rather easy task for a young man, but I wasn't so sure. I was almost 80.

But my urge to fish was strong. Fishing had been in my blood from my earliest years growing up in Clifton Forge, Virginia, where, during my teenage years, I became an avid angler, fishing mainly for bass and trout in rivers and creeks close to my hometown. The primary river I fished was a beautiful cool-water stream, the Cowpasture River in Allegheny County, where my targets were smallmouth bass, rock bass and bluegills. Occasionally my uncle Earl would take me to the Calfpasture River, a nearby stream similar to the Cowpasture but smaller. I considered both these streams my home waters when I was growing up.

After graduating high school, I worked five summers in Yellowstone National Park where I became even more addicted to fishing, specifically trout fishing, using a fly rod. I fished Yellowstone country and other locations in the Rockies, from New Mexico to Alberta, about 40 times over the past decades, drawn by the excellent trout fishing. A few days of fishing in the Rockies seemed to benefit my physical and mental health. I've referred to my love of fishing as a "fishing addiction" in my book "Turning Points."

Over the year before my invitation to fish the Calfpasture River, I had worked hard to improve my physical health in order to fish again. But prior years had brought a number of health issues. The year I retired from Clemson University at age 65, I was diagnosed with diabetes. At age 70, my health took another nosedive, first with kidney cancer which required removal of my left kidney, then with brain surgery to correct a condition called hydrocephalus, or fluid on the brain which caused me to stumble and fall when walking short distances. Surgery helped, but soon I was bent over and stumbling again with pain in my back. Surgery removed a spur from my lower spine but gave me only short-term relief. Further testing revealed I had a slipped disc and needed more surgery.

Damn, I was getting a little depressed! One surgery after another in a period of about six years. Would I ever be able to fish again?

Finally, I got some good news. The surgeon who performed my brain surgery came to my rescue. After studying the spinal tests, she recommended against further surgery, instead recommending a pain-management doctor who injected steroids into my spine. Within days I could stand upright and walk much farther without pain. With my core muscles weakened from my time dealing with debilitating pain, I had some catching up to do. I began to exercise until I was able to walk further and more frequently without pain.

From the previous year, when I had been forced to use a motorized scooter to get around, stooped from pain in my back and depressed from all the surgeries, I had made some remarkable progress. I thought I was fairly healthy for an old codger nearly 80 years old. I could stand and walk upright for considerable distances, and my mental outlook was much better. Why not try fishing? Fishing had been such an integral part of my life, and now, after about a 10-year hiatus, I thought I was ready to go fishing again!

*I was now able to hike with my friend of forty years, John Garton*

I was getting plenty of exercise. I felt good. It looked more and more like I would go back to my old home waters of the Calfpasture River.

But I began to have other qualms. It had been almost ten years since I seriously wet a line. Would the fire I had for fishing still burn in my veins? And if I went back to the Calfpasture, would the land — the forests, streams and wildlife — still be as I remembered it from so long ago? I had some doubts. It had been about 60 years since I had been to the Calfpasture, and just about everything in my world had dramatically changed during that time. It was hard to imagine the Calfpasture and its environment had not changed, too. I was determined to find out.

There were some logistical challenges. How would I get to Virginia? Rick's home was in Hanover County, Virginia, about 20 miles from Richmond, over 400 miles from Clemson, and I didn't drive anymore.

*Cole, me, Rick and Jud in our Clemson shirts at Rick's house just before the Florida State-Clemson game.*

It didn't take us long to solve that problem. Jud, who lives just outside Atlanta, would pick me up on the Saturday morning of Columbus Day weekend and drive us to Virginia. We would spend the night at Rick's house, get up early on Sunday and drive the three hours to the Calfpasture.

The Calfpasture is a small river that is more like a creek when the water is low. Virginia had been in a severe drought during the summer of 2019, and the river was low and clear, making the fish wary and difficult to catch, at least for me, but not so much for Rick, Jud and Cole, Rick's 18-year-old son. I started fishing with my fly rod, but my casting was so rusty and my vision so poor that often I couldn't detect strikes. I managed to catch a few fish on my fly rod, but soon saw the wisdom of Cole's suggestion that I might catch more fish if I switched to one of their spinning outfits.

*The Calfpasture River, low and clear during the droughty summer of 2019*

Thankfully, Cole took me under his wing, and, with his tutelage, I began to catch fish at a faster rate. Although my numbers were not impressive — nor was the size of the fish I caught — I did manage to catch a four-species "Calfpasture Grand Slam," as my companions called it: smallmouth bass, rock bass or redeye, redbreast sunfish and fallfish. The fallfish is actually a minnow that grows up to 20 inches in Virginia and is a hard fighter, and even though it is just a minnow, it earned its place as a component of the grand slam, according to Rick and Jud. So, I had a grand slam, and I didn't fall in the stream but once — it was more of a "slide-in" than fall-in when the bank gave way. Overall, not a bad performance for an old man who hadn't fished for almost 10 years.

*Cole with a 15-inch fallfish*     *Rich with a nice smallmouth bass*

The real fishermen, Rick, Jud and Cole, far out-fished me. But I enjoyed the companionship, the fishing and the beautiful environment immensely. After all, I was fishing with two of my favorite former students from about 30 years ago. Jud earned his Master of

Forest Resources in the late 1980s and Rick his Ph.D. in the early 1990s. And my new young friend, Cole, had willingly consented to be my guide, possibly because I tried to teach him some of the basics of fly tying on that Saturday evening at Rick's house. He caught on quickly, and with a little practice I am sure he will become an excellent fly tier. Rick had tutored Cole well in the art of fishing, and Cole was certainly an accomplished angler for his age.

What more could I have asked for? I was fishing with two good friends who after decades thought enough of me to invite me along. The weather was gorgeous, the land beautiful and hardly changed from how I remembered it long ago. Wildlife was abundant (we saw two bald eagles, a coyote, many songbirds and lots of deer), and the river had plenty of fish. The human population density was low, and there were no super-highways, no fast-food restaurants, no large urban areas — just the two small, peaceful country towns of Churchville and Deerfield. Modern society had not yet encroached on this idyllic rural environment. Here, along the Calfpasture, man and nature were in complete harmony, just as I remembered it from when I was a teenager.

Yes, I guess I did go home again, if only for a short time. The experience of fishing again where I had fished 60 years ago, with old friends and a young new friend in an absolutely beautiful environment, has rejuvenated me physically and mentally, making me think I could go on to 90, at least.

*The Calfpasture flows through private farmland in
the Ridge and Valley Province of Virginia*

# SPLASH

On a September morning in the fall of 2022, my new fishing friend, Allen, and I headed to the South Carolina mountains to fish the Chattooga and Chauga rivers. It would be the first time that I had seriously fished for trout in about 10 years, and I knew I would be rusty. My wife and I had been living in Clemson Downs, a retirement center, for 10 years. Some serious health issues had forced me to use a motorized scooter. But I hated using the scooter, and after embarking on a vigorous exercise program to help me recover my health, I had gotten rid of the scooter. I felt so much stronger and capable that I thought I could again wade the swift trout streams of mountainous South Carolina. I was eager to fish again.

Allen and I left Clemson at 7 a.m. on a Friday and drove to the Chattooga River, a whitewater river made famous in the movie "Deliverance." Allen is a novice fly fisherman, although he is a very experienced catfish and bass fisherman, while I have been a serious fly fisherman for about 60 years. Experience however, as you will see, is not everything. An old fly fisherman can still learn a few things from a novice fly fisherman.

We parked at a pull-off near the Burrells Ford bridge, put on our waders and geared up. It was a cool, beautiful morning, and the river was gorgeous, just what we hoped for. Two older gentlemen were at the bridge before us and indicated they were planning to fish upstream of the bridge, so Allen and I hiked up a fisherman's path to get well above them. We began fishing a series of riffles and pools, Allen using a small wet fly with a green body and me a #14 hare's ear nymph.

*The Chattooga where I made the biggest splash of the day*

Allen soon caught a small rainbow trout — his first trout ever on a fly — but I was having no luck on my nymph. After fishing for an hour or so with only one fish between us, we decided to drive over to the Chauga River to give that stream a try. Allen found information on his cell phone that the South Carolina Department of Natural Resources had recently stocked that river.

But first, I had to get out of the Chattooga. I was wading in swift water about three feet deep trying to find a "get-out" spot. The river bottom was slick as ice, and the rubber soles on my wading boots didn't help stabilize me. Suddenly, I was out of control. Before I knew it, there was a huge splash, and I was horizontal in the river, mostly underwater and being pushed rapidly downstream by the swift current. Half of my fishing hat and the hearing aid in my right ear were the only parts of me that escaped the dunking. Thankfully, the water was deep enough that I didn't land on a rock and break a hip.

I have been wading trout streams for over 60 years, during which time I have occasionally slipped and fallen in, but on only one other occasion — on Abrams Creek in the Smokies — have I so completely immersed myself and been swept downstream. The cold water was refreshing, but I wasn't there to be refreshed! I frantically tried to grab a rock or anything I could grasp to keep from being swept further downstream. Finally, I caught a rock on the river bottom and my legs swung below me. Now I was able to get my feet under me and stand up. Of course, I was completely soaked. The blue jeans I was wearing under my waders were sopping wet, as was my flannel shirt, and my waders were half full of water.

Allen was upstream, around a bend in the river, so he did not see my amazing lack of dexterity as I floundered in the river. But he soon heard me hollering his name as I tried to regain my balance and get to the bank. He hurriedly came down and helped me out of the river.

Even though it was a cool morning my chest waders kept my body heat in, and I soon began to feel comfortable, despite the wet clothes. Allen offered me a dry shirt, but I declined. After a few minutes, we decided to take the 15-minute drive over to one of his favorite fishing spots on the Chauga River. The Chauga is a beautiful trout stream and once, before Lake Jocassee was created, held the record for the largest brown trout caught in the state — nine pounds.

From the parking area on the Chauga, we hiked down a short, but steep, rocky road to the river to see if we could find any evidence that the fish-stocking truck had recently been there. We saw tracks of a 4-wheel-drive vehicle leading right into the river, which we assumed meant that the stocking truck had been there. So, we hiked back up to the truck to get our fishing gear. (Why hadn't we taken our equipment down to the river in the first place?) This uphill hike was not so easy for me with my wet jeans and some water still in my waders, but finally we got geared up and hiked back down to the river.

Soon, Allen started catching fish regularly. I noticed that he had changed whatever was on the end of his line. Knowing that Allen was not averse to using live bait, I assumed he was now using an earthworm, or a "garden hackle," as fly fishermen know them.

I swallowed my pride and asked him what he was using for bait. To my surprise, he was using a small plastic worm called a honey worm. It looked like an inchworm or mealworm and had a nasty smell — to me, but apparently not to the trout.

I asked Allen if I could "borrow" one of his honey worms, and he said, "How much is it worth to you?"

I replied, "Well, it's been almost 10 years since I have caught a trout, so I'll pay whatever you ask, as long as it's not more than a dollar."

He laughed and pulled one of his secret weapons from a small jar and impaled it onto the #12 hook on the end of my leader. I thanked him, moved downstream a bit and began casting into a nice riffle-pool where he had already caught a couple of trout. The honey worm was like a weighted nymph, so I didn't have any trouble casting it.

After just a few casts, I had a strike and hooked a 10-inch rainbow trout — my first trout in about a decade! I didn't care that it was a stocked trout. I was just happy to be a successful trout fisherman again. I soon caught another rainbow of about the same size, and Allen caught a few more in the pool above me.

It was now about 3:30 in the afternoon, and we were both pretty beat. Allen was 75 years old, and I was 81 at the time of this excursion. An 8½-hour trout fishing trip was about enough for us.

On our way home, I told Allen that this might just be my last trout fishing trip. "I am an old man now, and my balance leaves a lot to be desired," I said.

Allen bristled and said, "What are you talking about? You can't let a little dip in the river stop you from doing something you love."

I've learned from Allen, an ex-Marine, that Marines never give up.

"You are probably right, Allen," I told him. "I will be ready to go again whenever you give me the word. The next time though, I am going to have some wading shoes with felt soles, like you have on yours. No more slip-sliding and splashing for me."

*The Chauga River where I recently caught my first trout in ten years*

We both agreed that we had had a great time and that we would soon go again. In the meantime, Allen, an electrician by trade, went to Florida to help restore power to areas devastated by Hurricane Ian. Quite a man!

Back at Clemson Downs, I went to my exercise class the following Monday. I jokingly told my wonderful exercise leader, Ana Oleyo, that she could expect to receive a summons to appear in court soon as I was suing her for breach of contract! After all Ana had been helping me with my balance for about a year to get me ready for my first trout fishing outing. She had put me through all kinds of obstacle courses to help me keep my balance, and if I lost my balance and she had to catch me, we always shouted, "SPLASH!" I had warned her that if I lost my balance while wading and fell in, I would have no choice but to sue her.

Ana replied good naturedly that it wasn't her fault that I fell in. She said I would have to take most of the blame because I forget to come to her balance class about half the time, and the classes I missed were the ones that would have kept me upright.

"How can you have good balance when you don't come to class?" she asked. She was right, of course, so I have no one to sue!

In the meantime, I will keep working with Ana on my balance and look forward to my next trout fishing trip. I have learned over the decades that a big part of the trout fishing experience is the anticipation of what comes next. Who knows? I might catch a big one next time and not even fall in!

# STUCK!!

Recently, I had the opportunity to go fishing with a new fishing buddy, Tom, in the Chauga River, one of my old fishing grounds. At 82 years old, with some health and balance problems, I had not done any serious fly fishing for a decade or so. To be honest, I had tried a couple of times to do serious trout fishing, but it was chiefly just fishing — not catching.

On this day in June 2023, I was determined that I would catch some fish. After all, I had been a fly fisherman since I had worked in Yellowstone Park during my college years. I'm not claiming that I am an expert, but with that many years of experience, I had learned to be a pretty good fly fisherman.

No one else was around when Tom and I began fishing at about eight that morning. We split up and were about 30 yards apart when I waded out into a nice pool with a good riffle flowing into it. I noticed as I was wading out that the bottom felt a bit like quicksand. It was a muddy mess of silt and decomposed leaves about a foot deep. With difficulty, I waded through the muck until I was on a solid rocky bottom.

"Wow," I thought. "A person, especially an old, unbalanced fisherman, could almost get stuck in this muck and have a hard time getting out." Little did I realize what was about to happen to me in just a few hours.

At the first fishing hole, I caught a rainbow and a brown trout, both about 10 inches long, on a #12 wet fly that had not yet been soaked enough to sink. The trout hit while the fly was floating on the surface. "This is fun!" I thought. Finally, I was going to catch some fish on a fishing trip.

Tom and I moved downstream to a nice riffle, and I caught several more trout, including a nice 12-inch brookie and a few rainbows and browns about the same size as my first two. I knew that they were all "stockers," but they still fought hard and were fun to catch.

The Chauga River has trout that are the result of both natural reproduction and what are called "hold-over trout" — stocked trout that survive for multiple years. While in the past I have caught browns in the Chauga up to 20 inches long which fit in both those categories, I don't believe any of the 10 fish I caught on this day were hold-overs.

Motivated by my success, I kept moving downstream and found one beautiful hole that was loaded with trout. There, I caught five more rainbows and browns. By now, I was getting a little tired and decided that I had about enough fishing for this day. I started wading back upstream to our starting point where I would wait for Tom.

Wading against the current was tough on this old-timer, and when I reached our put-in spot, I was "about whipped." But fishermen always want to have just one more cast, so I began wading out to where I had caught my first two fish that day. I was thinking about fish; I wasn't thinking about having to wade through that mucky bottom again.

*The Chauga River, where I got stuck in the muck*

Before I knew it, I was stuck in that muck. The longer I stood there, with muck and mud up to my shins, the more stuck I became. Now I couldn't even take a step. Perhaps it was because I was so tired that I couldn't move, but mainly it was because this was the stickiest stuff I had ever stepped in. This muck actually created a suction, holding my feet with a greater force than I could muster to lift them out.

So, there I was — stuck with no one around to help me out of my predicament. I twisted around, but I could twist just from the waist up — my feet wouldn't move. Suddenly I lost my balance and fell over backwards in that disgusting muck and mud. I felt water and muck rapidly entering my chest waders, my clothes were soaking wet from neck to toes, and my feet were still stuck in the muck. What a hell of a predicament! I couldn't move.

The more I struggled, the stucker (Is that even a word?) I got. I was in no danger of drowning; the water was too shallow for that. I finally convinced myself to just relax and slowly begin to work my boots up and out of this goo. Inch by inch, while lying on my back and weighted down by water-filled waders, I began to free my feet. "Now," I thought, "I will just roll over and crawl out of here."

"Not so fast," the muck seemed to say. I could not roll over. There were air pockets in the bottoms of my waders that floated my legs up to the surface. It felt like someone was holding my legs up so that I couldn't turn over. What frustration! Here I was, still stuck in the mud and muck, and even after finally freeing my feet, I still couldn't turn over and crawl out of this mess.

Finally, I calmed myself down enough to think about my situation. I still had my wading staff attached to my waist. "Perhaps," I thought, "I can use it to pry myself up so that I can roll over." It was certainly worth a try, and it worked! Now I was on my elbows and knees — but still stuck in this muck. I still couldn't crawl out to the bank. This stuff was the stickiest s**t I'd ever experienced. Excuse me, but by now, you know how I was feeling!

Thankfully, I noticed a single rock sticking about six inches out of the water just beyond my reach. I finally managed to get a grip on it and pulled myself to it, tearing a piece of my thumbnail during the process. I just lay there, horizontal, in the water, hugging that rock, and rested. I was still too tired and weak from all the effort I had exerted to crawl to and up the bank. Plus, it felt like I had 50 pounds of water in my waders. My legs weren't strong enough to haul all that weight onto the bank.

*An artist's rendering of my predicament*

What a mess I had gotten myself into. In 60+ years of trout fishing, I had never had anything like this to happen to me. I have fished many streams all over the country that had pockets of deep sand that might get you stuck, including certain sections of the Madison River, which the angling writer Charlie Brooks said he would not fish for any amount of money. Well, I had fished that river and never got so stuck that I fell over backwards and couldn't get up. No, this Chauga muck was a new experience for me and one I don't anticipate will happen to this old codger again.

Finally, as I was lying attached to that wonderful rock, I saw a young man walking toward me. I shouted, "Help me!" He hustled down to the water's edge and took my fishing rod and wading staff, put them up on the bank, and reached down to offer me his hand. With his help, I was able to climb onto the bank and take a much-needed break — and empty my waders.

I thanked the young man profusely. He said his name was Jerry, and he lived just a few miles down the road. I was extremely grateful. If Jerry hadn't come along when he did, I would have probably still been lying in the water when Tom came back to check on me. I wondered if I would have been alive — or dead from exhaustion. I expect I would have been alive, but certainly very exhausted.

It may be that this was my last trout fishing trip. If it was, it was a good one. I caught 14 fish: 11 trout, including rainbows, browns and a nice brookie, plus two bluehead chubs, and one bluegill. The weather was perfect, and I was fishing with a good friend. But what will always make this trip most memorable to me is the experience of getting my feet stuck in the muck, falling backwards in the horrible stuff, then getting my whole body stuck in that gooey mess and spending about 15 minutes practically immobilized in the muck.

Later, when I told my friends, Allen and Tom, about what happened, they both said that they'd had almost the same experience at the very same spot! Allen said that he, too, fell when his feet got stuck, but he didn't fall backwards so he was able to remove himself to a more solid spot.

I think I might suggest to the South Carolina Department of Natural Resources that they put a big sign in this muck saying **"Danger: Quicksand. Fish at Your Own Risk — Especially Unbalanced Old Timers."**

# AN OLD-TIMERS LOVE STORY

Back in 1978, I was a 37-year-old bachelor living in Clemson, South Carolina, with my best friend, Doc, a two-year-old Basset Hound. My dad had died the year before, so I invited my mom, who had a weak heart resulting from childhood rheumatic fever, to leave Clifton Forge, Virginia, to come live with Doc and me.

I had been hired as an associate professor in 1971 in the Department of Forest Resources at Clemson University to teach silviculture — what I call applied forest ecology — and to conduct silvicultural research related to forest resources. It was a demanding, wonderful job perfectly suited for me, and I immersed myself in it.

But I was a lonely man. I was thirty-seven years old, never been married and had really never had any serious girlfriends. So, there I was, an associate professor in the Department of Forest Resources with a great job, living with my mother and a basset hound named Doc in a new house that mom and I had just bought.

How did I get from there to here? It's all because of Carolyn.

We met courtesy of Doc.

Soon after my mom, Doc and I moved into our new house, Doc and I were out in the front yard, thinking about how "we" could landscape it to make it more attractive. Suddenly, Doc took off, dashing at breakneck speed — breakneck speed for a basset hound with a lame front leg. He raced across the street without looking to see if traffic was coming, and headed straight for a young lady and her daughter who were walking down the sidewalk on the other side of the street.

Doc was completely infatuated with these two ladies, and they seemed to feel the same about him. I followed as fast as I could to get Doc under control and introduce myself to my neighbors. I will never forget this first meeting with Carolyn and Melanie. Carolyn was wearing a bright yellow jumpsuit that fit her to a tee, if you know what I mean. I told her my mom and I had recently moved into the house across the street and asked her where she lived. She said, "Right here," and pointed to a nice brick house just across the street. Carolyn was 35 years old, married, with two children, Chris and Melanie. She had married young, at age 19, and dropped out of Lander College after two years to take care of a growing family.

I had never met a woman like Carolyn. Not only was she beautiful, but she was a great conversationalist as well. And so empathetic. She seemed to understand why I was still a bachelor, and she seemed to admire the fact that I had asked mom to move in with me when my dad died.

I was likewise empathetic to her situation. She was going through a rough divorce, had two children, no work experience outside the home and was living on the small alimony settlement she received. I could understand that she needed some company to help her make it through her tough times.

"Would you have dinner with me tomorrow night?" I blurted out. "I believe we've got a lot to talk about."

Wow, did I actually say that? I have always been so shy around women, but I was so taken with Carolyn, it just seemed like it was now or never. I couldn't let this wonderful woman get away.

"I would love to go with you," she said. "But my divorce is not final yet, so I don't think I should. When it's final, I'll let you know, and we can go out then."

"Darn," I thought. "That's the story of my love life — always something that prevents a romance from blossoming. This time, it's a divorce that's not finalized. Maybe I'm just supposed to stay single."

While romance and the love of a woman had always been elusive for me, I will have to admit that I had never tried that hard to win a woman's heart. My life had been consumed by studying and trying to excel through ten years of college at Hampden-Sydney, Virginia Tech and the University of Idaho pursuing B.S., M.S. and Ph.D. degrees, followed by a post-doctorate position at the University of Florida, and then teaching and research at Clemson for seven years. I had little time for courting.

But now I had met Carolyn, and there was hope. After all, she did say that she would go out with me when her divorce was final. Hopefully, that wouldn't be too far in the future.

About a month later, I saw her walking again, and this time she told me that her divorce was final. Now she could go out with me. The following Friday we went to El Matador in Greenville, the oldest Mexican restaurant in South Carolina. We had so much to talk about that the management almost had to run us out as closing time approached.

To say I was smitten with Carolyn would be a gross understatement. I adored her right from that first date, and she seemed to be very fond of me. We started dating on a very frequent basis, usually going to a restaurant for dinner, or to a movie or a ride into the mountains. I especially remember our second date. We went to Vince Perone's Italian restaurant in Greenville and had another wonderful time. As we left the restaurant and got in my car, I decided it was time for me to give her a sweet kiss.

Wow, did she "lay one on me!" I had never been kissed like that! It excited me so much that I drove off the curb as we left the parking lot. After that, Carolyn and I would go out for lunch almost every day. We enjoyed each other's company so much. And as Johnny Cash sang in "The Ring of Fire," "the flame burned higher." We were deeply in love, but there was one test of our devotion to each other still to come.

Before I met Carolyn, I had applied for and been granted a sabbatical from Clemson to write a book. I decided to work on my book in Yellowstone National Park where — wouldn't you know it — I could fish in the afternoons after writing for a half day. But the question was whether Carolyn would wait for me while I was gone or find another man? I knew other men had their eyes on her.

I was lucky to find a modest, affordable cabin in West Yellowstone, Montana, where I could work. Thankfully, there was a phone booth a half block from my cabin, and I almost wore that phone out, calling Carolyn every evening and talking with her for up to an hour at a time. Many a tourist no doubt drove by that phone booth and wondered, "When the hell is he going to get off that phone? He's been on it for an hour!"

*My new family: Carolyn, Chris and Melanie*

Well, we passed that separation test with flying colors. Absence did make our hearts grow fonder, so instead of staying in Yellowstone for six months as I had originally planned, I cut my sabbatical short and went home after just three months. There was no way I was going to stay away from Carolyn for six months!

Our courtship lasted nine months, and we married December 27, 1978.

Doc and I moved across the street to Carolyn's house and mom stayed in our previous house. I was fortunate to be able to persuade my sister, Kitty, to come live with mom. After teaching high school German in Virginia Beach, Virginia, for 25 years, Kitty was a little burned out. She was still single, and easily persuaded to come live with mom.

After we married, Carolyn enrolled in Clemson University and earned her B.A. in elementary education in 1988. After graduation, she got a job as an elementary education teacher at Morrison Elementary in Clemson where the students loved her.

I continued to teach silviculture, forest protection and fire ecology at Clemson for 35 years until I retired in 2005. I also had a very active research program, authoring about 150 technical and scientific papers and supervising the programs of 45 graduate students.

Our love has flourished for 45 years. We have seldom had any major disagreements or arguments, probably because we liked so many of the same things such as country music, dining out and taking mini-vacations to the Rocky Mountains or the Southern Appalachians. We were so compatible that there was nothing to argue about in our relationship.

Carolyn has always been tolerant of my addiction to fishing, especially fly fishing. While most wives would probably have divorced me, Carolyn encouraged me to fish because she knew my passion for it helped keep me on an even keel. I have battled cyclothymia — a mild form of bipolar disorder that is part of my family history — all my adult life, and fishing helped me through the occasional depressions I would experience.

When Carolyn and I reached our 70s and began experiencing some serious health problems, we decided it would be best if we moved into a retirement village called Clemson Downs. Carolyn had battled breast cancer, which thankfully was cured with radiation. And I experienced a quick succession of serious health issues.

Sadly, after about five years here at the Downs, Carolyn had to go to the Health Care facility. Neither our wonderful caregiver nor I was able to take care of her hygiene, balance and memory problems although we tried.

Still, I make the short walk to the health care facility every day to visit Carolyn (except during the COVID lockdown). Carolyn gets great care and is content, as am I. For us, Clemson Downs has been the best place we could be. The administration and staff are wonderful, and we love the activities for residents. On Valentine's Day every year, we go to the Clemson Downs party and have a grand time. Every Wednesday evening, we go to the Bistro, a small restaurant on the Downs campus for what we call our "date night." We also go out for dinner about once every two weeks, thanks to our caregiver.

Carolyn always wears a pretty bow in her hair, trying, I think, to look pretty for me. I appreciate that and still think she is beautiful, although she denies it.

On a recent Wednesday, we had a special night at the Bistro. It was early in the evening and the crowds had not shown up yet. We were the only people there. Two very sweet young waitresses were taking care of our needs. As we were finishing our meal, I asked them if they would like to hear Carolyn sing "I'll Fly Away," one of her favorite songs. They were delighted, and said, "Yes, please do."

Carolyn has a beautiful voice, and as she began to sing, one of the ladies who later told us she was in her church's choir, chimed in and sang with her. They sounded so good together. We all clapped our hands when the song was over. It made Carolyn almost cry. Me, too.

I then asked if they would like to hear Carolyn sing "Amazing Grace." "Oh, yes," they said. So, Carolyn sang that song beautifully and got another round of applause from us. She cried a little — tears of joy, for sure. It made me so proud of her and love her even more. Here she is, having been confined to a wheelchair for over five years, and she still has the spirit to want to make others happy. What a woman!

Our love is just as strong now, after 45 years of marriage, as it was decades ago, maybe even stronger. We have been through tough times together, as have all marriages, but our love always pulled us through. Now we are looking forward to what the next decade of our lives will bring. We are positive in our outlook that there will still be many good times, and these two old love birds will be able to handle whatever life throws our way.

*Carolyn and me at the 2022 Valentine's Day party*

# THE INCREDIBLE MARY DRAPER INGLES

In July 1755, Mary Draper Ingles and her husband Will were living in a small village of just a few families called Draper's Meadow, Virginia. It was the westernmost settlement in America at the time, just east of the Allegheny Mountains.

Mary Draper Ingles is my fifth-great grandmother, and this is her story.

Mary and Will had two children, Thomas, age 4, and George, age 2. Mary was expecting their third child at any time. Although the Ingles family was living in Indian territory, they had never experienced problems with any of the Native American tribes. Occasionally the Ingles saw Shawnee war parties from the Ohio area passing through to do battle with the Cherokees and Catawbas, southern tribes, but they had never been a threat to villagers in Draper's Meadow.

However, recently things had begun to change. During what was known as the French and Indian War (1754-1763), France and

England were engaged in a bitter conflict for control of the Ohio River Valley. The French in the area primarily moved along the rivers trapping and trading without creating permanent settlements. The English generally were farmers who settled permanently, displacing the Native Americans. The Shawnees saw the threat of the English settlers to their lands and, siding with the French, began conducting raids on English settlements such as Draper's Meadows.

On a late-July morning, Mary was doing household chores and taking care of her young children. All day she had been nervous and anxious with the feeling of impending danger. To add to her anxiety, her husband Will and his brother-in-law, John, were some distance away working in their grain fields.

Mary's sister-in-law, Betty, who lived nearby, had been washing clothes at their well and was walking back to her cabin when she saw a band of Shawnees approaching in what she took to be a very hostile manner. Running inside her cabin, she screamed an alarm and grabbed her small baby from the cradle. As Betty ran out the other side of the cabin, she felt a sharp pain causing her to drop the baby as her arm was shattered by a musket ball. The attackers immediately captured her and cruelly killed her baby by bashing its head against one of the cabin's logs as the mother watched.

Mary and her two children were also taken captive, as was a neighbor, Henry Lenard. In the same attack, Mary's mother, Eleanor, was killed and scalped, along with several others. The surviving captives were tied together for a long march — everyone except for pregnant Mary, who was placed on a horse and allowed to ride. The captors and their captives followed Sinking Creek to the New

River and then headed west, following a series of rivers back to their Shawnee village in Ohio.

On the second night away from Draper's Meadows, the party of warriors and captives camped on top of a cliff above the New River with steep drop-offs on three sides. Mary would remember this stop, not only for its intimidating presence but because it was here that Mary was allowed to make a splint for Betty's broken arm.

The next night, with Betty's help, Mary gave birth to a baby girl who she named Bettie Eleanor and called Eleanor. When the next morning came, after no delay for rest and recovery, Mary was put back on horseback to continue the journey with the baby in her arms. Suffering from dizziness, nausea and pain, Mary rode on, covering her clothes and the horse she was riding with her blood.

For 30 days, the captors and captives marched first along the New River, then the Kanawha River, and finally, the Ohio River. At the mouth of the Scioto River, a major tributary of the Ohio, they came to what Mary, whose only frame of reference was tiny Draper's Meadow, called a large Shawnee village. The captives spent the night tied to posts, and the next morning were gathered to unwillingly participate in what was called "running the gauntlet," a form of torture which forced captives to run between two lines of Indians who beat them with sticks, switches and clubs as they ran. To be allowed to survive, captives had to make it all the way to the finish line. If they fell, they had to start over again. If they failed, they were killed. Mary's neighbor, Henry Lenard, and her sister-in-law, Betty, were viciously beaten and barely completed the gauntlet.

Mary was not forced to run the gauntlet. The young chief of the raiding party, a warrior named Captain Wildcat, persuaded the tribe to spare her from running the gauntlet. He admired Mary's bravery and dignity, and how she had handled the ordeal of giving birth and caring for a baby on the long trek back to the Shawnee village.

During the three months Mary was with the Shawnees, she made friends with an old Dutch woman named Ghetel who had been captured in Pennsylvania. Ghetel had survived the gauntlet, and her toughness had gained the respect of her captors.

During the late summer of her captivity, Mary's two sons, Thomas and George, were taken to another Shawnee village by Captain Wildcat. Her newborn, Eleanor, was also taken from her to become the daughter of an Indian woman who had recently lost her own child.

Mary found herself childless, far from home and living with cruel people who had shown little respect for human life. She feared for her own safety every day.

After several weeks at the Shawnee village, Mary and Ghetel were given more freedom and allowed to go out and forage for nuts, grapes, berries and other edibles to feed the village. The Shawnee thought there was no chance that these two women would be foolish enough to try to escape. They believed the women's homes were too far away, they would have little to eat, and there were dangerous wild animals such as wolves, bears and panthers along the way.

Late that summer, two French trappers who lived with the Shawnee, Goulart and LaPlante, along with about a dozen warriors, took Mary and Ghetel four days west of the main village, further along the Ohio River, to a natural saltlick to mine salt for the tribe. The saltlick, now called Big Bone Lick State Historic Site, was on the Kentucky side of the river and got its name from the fossilized bones of Pleistocene mammoths, mastodons and other animals that had come there to lick salt.

Mary thought constantly of escaping. But, she reasoned, even if she could persuade Ghetel to go with her, what chance would she and the old Dutch woman have to successfully make it back to Draper's Meadows? Eleanor was nearby. The Indian woman who had taken her baby was at the saltlick with Mary still caring for Eleanor as if she were her own baby. But Mary knew that even if she could get Eleanor away from the woman and escape, the baby could not survive the long trek home.

Weighing her choices, Mary decided that any chance, no matter how small, was better than staying with the savages who had killed and scalped her mother, killed Betty's infant baby, taken her sons away and burned alive two white captives at the Shawnee village.

Mary made the agonizing decision to leave her little baby and attempt an escape.

During their two weeks at the saltlick, the French traders had allowed Mary and Ghetel to go out into the woods to forage for food. Goulart even loaned the women his tomahawk so they could cut branches bearing fruit or nuts and mark trees to help find their way back to the camp. Mary and Ghetel decided that now was the time. On one of these forays, they would escape. So, one day, armed only with two wool blankets, the tomahawk, and the flimsy, shredded dresses on their backs, they went out to forage — and never returned.

Mary's only escape plan was to follow the same rivers they had followed when they were taken to the Shawnee village. This time, however, they would be going upstream against the current. She knew that eventually the rivers would take her home, but were she and Ghetel up to this journey? What would they eat? Would they be killed by wild animals? Would they be recaptured by Indian war parties moving along the same rivers? Would they get lost in this vast, uncharted wilderness?

Mary could not read or write, but she had forced herself during the journey out to the Shawnee village in Ohio to memorize landmarks along the way. She reasoned that when she escaped, as she knew she would, she would be able to recognize her way back home.

From the saltlick on the Kentucky side of the Ohio River back to her home and her husband Will was about 450 miles — as the crow flies. But there was no such direct route. To add to their complications, neither Mary nor Ghetel could swim. When they came to a large tributary, they would often have to walk upstream for miles, or even tens of miles, to find a shallow that they could wade across. Then they would walk back downstream to the main river. These excursions essentially doubled the distance they had to travel. Geographers estimate that their 450-mile journey back to Draper's Meadows was more like 900 miles.

It was late September when Mary and Ghetel escaped, and they faced the approaching winter with only tattered dresses and shoes and two wool blankets for warmth. While they had the Frenchman's tomahawk, they had no food except what they could find: nuts, fruits like grapes and pawpaws, roots, and other plants that they had no way of identifying as toxic. Some of the plants made them severely ill with nausea and diarrhea. To survive, they began eating earthworms and grubs that they found under rocks.

For six weeks, Mary and Ghetel struggled through this wilderness, miraculously avoiding Indian war parties returning from raids on settlements to the south, but desperately hungry. Near the end of their journey, driven mad by starvation, Ghetel had twice tried to kill and eat Mary. Mary was able to fight off her attacks and to move ahead of her. Eventually, Mary found an Indian canoe hidden under brush by the river and was able to cross the river. Now she felt safe from the old Dutch woman.

As Mary approached the New River narrows, the most challenging terrain of her journey home, she came to an area of huge cliffs, some hundreds of feet high, that plunged straight down to the river. Deep water along the river's edge meant that in order for her to continue she would have to climb the cliffs and then crawl and slide down the other side. She was exhausted, starving and nearly frozen to death, but she forced herself to go on. The last cliff proved to be the most difficult. But she knew she had to climb it. The river was just too deep for her to wade.

After spending half of a day crawling and climbing 300 feet to the top of the cliff, Mary recognized it as the place where she had made a splint for Betty's broken arm on the second day of their captivity. She knew she was only about 30 miles from home and her beloved Will. But would her body let her go on? "Yes," she told herself, "even if it's the last thing I do."

Mary crawled and slid down the more gently sloping side of the cliff and plodded on to flatter terrain. She couldn't give up now.

Finally, six weeks after escaping from captivity, Mary was almost home. As she crawled along, she saw smoke coming from a cabin that she recognized as belonging to one of her neighbors, Adam Harmon. Adam and his two sons were working in their corn field when they heard a feeble voice calling their names. Then they saw a frail, thin woman, almost naked, with totally white hair, crawling through the corn stalks toward them.

Adam and his sons ran to her, barely recognizing the woman as Mary. She was a mere bundle of bones. They carried her limp and fragile body to their cabin and gradually nursed her back to health. After she was strong enough to travel, the Harmons took her to the small Dunkard's Bottom Fort near Draper's Meadows where she and Will were joyfully united at last.

Mary, however, felt unsafe at this fort. Indian raids were still occurring in the New River valley, so she pleaded with Will to take her further east to a larger fort, Fort Vass, near present-day Roanoke. Still suffering from her trauma and having nightmares about her ordeal, Mary didn't feel safe there either. She begged Will to take her farther east to an even larger fort in present-day Bedford County, Virginia. The move was fortuitous. The day after they left, Fort Vass was attacked by Shawnee warriors, and all the fort's inhabitants were either killed or taken captive.

In Bedford County, Mary slowly recovered her health, and the following spring, she and Will returned to Draper's Meadows. There they set up a successful ferry business on the New River carrying the ever-growing number of settlers across the river. She and Will had four more children, three girls and a boy, John Ingles, Sr., who later wrote what is considered to be the most accurate account of Mary's harrowing journey. Amazingly, the old Dutch woman, Ghetel, who escaped with Mary, also made it back to Draper's Meadow, and legend has it, was able to eventually travel back to her home in Pennsylvania.

Will died at age 53 but Mary lived on to the age of 83, another 60 years after her capture and epic escape from the Shawnees. She never remarried.

In 1768, when he was 17 years old, Mary's oldest son, Thomas, who had been captured with her, was ransomed from the Shawnees with the aid of friendly Cherokees. Her youngest son, George, had died shortly after Captain Wildcat took him from his mother to another Shawnee village. The baby, Bettie Eleanor, who had been adopted by the Shawnee woman was never heard from again.

Mary's incredible story is one of a young farm woman who possessed uncommon courage, bravery, determination and toughness — characteristics that enabled her to escape captivity by the Shawnees and travel almost a thousand miles on foot, with no provisions, to return to her home. It is a testimony to toughness, determination and resourcefulness that has been told and retold for generations.

**NOTE:** Mary Draper Ingles' story of capture and escape from the Shawnee Indians during the French and Indian War exists in a number of legends that vary in their specific details. For this story, I relied heavily on the fictional novel "Follow the River" by best-selling author, James Alexander Thom, along with the corroborating story "Escape from Indian Captivity: The Story of Mary Draper Ingles and Son Thomas Ingles as Told by John Ingles, Sr.," edited by Roberta Ingles Steele and Andrew Lewis Ingles as the basis for my retelling of this story. It is through John Ingles, Sr. the youngest of Mary and Will's seven children that I am descended. John had heard his mother talk of her harrowing ordeal for decades before she died in 1815.

A number of places in and around the site of Mary's saga honor her even today: New River Gorge National Park and Preserve near Glen Jean, West Virginia; Mary Draper Inglis Trail in Radford, Virginia; and the homestead of William and Mary Ingles where they operated a ferry across the New River in Radford, Virginia, is still a working farm, open periodically to the public.

# THE CLEMSON EXPERIMENTAL FOREST: THE POWER OF CONSERVATION

At 17,500 acres, the Clemson Experimental Forest almost surrounds the Clemson University campus, stretching along Lake Hartwell and extending into both Pickens and Anderson counties. During my years as a professor of forestry at Clemson, I grew to think of the forest as a constant inspiration. It was my outdoor classroom; it was home to the research projects of my graduate students; it was on my route to school every day; and it fueled my passion for forestry, allowing me to enhance my performance as a teacher and researcher.

I am certainly not unbiased in my view of the Clemson Experimental Forest. I care a great deal about this beautiful land. But I am not alone. It is one of the most beloved features of the South Carolina piedmont and a treasured part of Clemson University. But it was not always a flourishing, thriving refuge for flora and fauna.

Today's forest is a forest resurrected, re-born from the efforts of man and the bounty of nature.

The forest began its new life thanks to the New Deal, a massive effort to lift America out of the Great Depression. President Franklin D. Roosevelt initiated a series of programs in the 1930s that included an "alphabet soup" of efforts such as the CCC (Civilian Conservation Corps), WPA (Works Progress Administration), CWA (Civil Works Administration), and NIRA (National Industrial Recovery Act). The New Deal programs had far-ranging and long-term effects that, as in the case of the Clemson Experimental Forest, we benefit from still today.

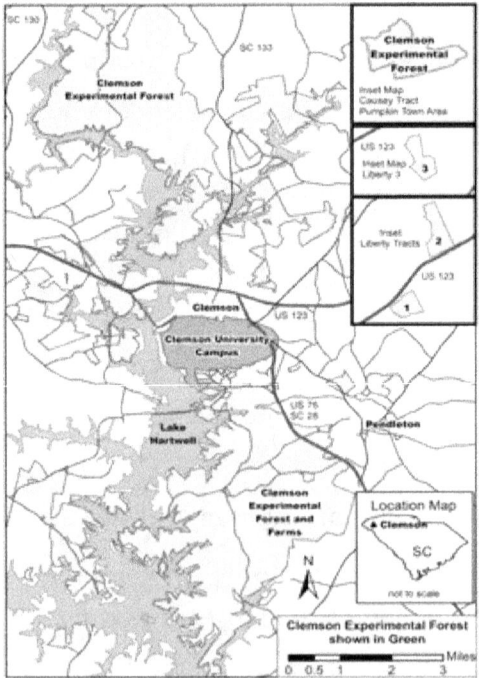

*The 17,500-acre Clemson Experimental Forest*

As part of the revitalization initiatives of the New Deal, federal funds were allocated to purchase eroded and marginal farmlands throughout the country and restore them to a productive use. Many thousands of acres of this type of depleted land covered the upper piedmont of South Carolina at the time.

Thanks to the efforts of George Aull, a Clemson University professor of agricultural economics, the federal government purchased approximately 27,000 acres of submarginal land surrounding the university and the city of Clemson in the early 1930s. In 1939, the government leased the land to the university to be managed for restoration and preservation of natural resources.

Clemson worked with the CCC and the WPA to plant millions of trees and to build bridges, dams, roads and other structures on the leased lands. Then, in 1954, apparently satisfied with the progress Clemson was making in restoring the land, the federal government deeded the property to the university with the provision that the lands could not be commercially developed — they were to be used for conservation, education and recreation. If the university were to use the lands for commercial development, they would revert to the federal government.

What followed were decades of enlightened forest management under the guidance of forest managers, beginning with Norbert Goebel who was hired by the university in 1947. Goebel was followed by a number of foresters, including Larry Reamer, Knight Cox and Russell Hardee. Under the guidance of these men, the lands have been transformed from eroded farmland to productive forest lands of great natural beauty and diversity. Perhaps most surprisingly, the experimental forest substantially pays for itself through sustainable timber harvests. Clemson University does not contribute significantly to fund the management and maintenance of the forest.

*The Clemson Experimental Forest is now a productive forest of great natural beauty and biodiversity*

*Timber harvest pays for most of the costs of managing the forest*

The wise management of the forest means that even though timber is harvested annually to pay most of the costs of management and maintenance, the volume of timber in the forest continues to increase decade by decade. In other words, every decade the volume growth of the forest continues to exceed the volume of timber cut so that the forest is truly sustainable.

The management objectives for the forest are to produce a never-ending supply of renewable resources — timber, wildlife, water and recreation — and provide unmatched opportunities for education and research. Clemson is indeed fortunate to own the 17,500-acre experimental forest. (Another 10,000 acres of the original purchase are in university farmland.) It is the nation's largest university-owned forest that is adjacent to its campus.

*Clemson University with the experimental forest in the background*

Other efforts to maintain and improve the forest include the practice of prescribed burning. These carefully planned and controlled burns are used to improve wildlife habitat, reduce flammable fuel, recycle nutrients and enhance biodiversity. Foresters also use thinning, improvement cuttings and herbicides to control forest stand composition and density while reducing the presence of undesirable invasive plants.

Natural areas, such as rock outcrops and waterfalls, as well as riparian zones and critical habitats of rare or unique plant communities are given special consideration before any management activities are prescribed that might affect them.

Within the forest are at least ten waterfalls, all easily accessible, 200 miles of permanent streams and foothills that rise over 300 feet above Lake Hartwell. The stunning natural beauty of the forest ensures the popularity of this natural resource with both the university and the general public.

This success is all a result of careful conservation. Conservation may be defined as "wise use without abuse." That simplistic definition includes the massive efforts of forest management. Smart forest management has not only restored trees to the once almost barren landscape of the 1930s, it has also restored plant diversity to the area as well. Now, over 750 species of plants, including 50 species of shrubs, eight species of orchids, 54 species of trees and 17 species of vines, call the forest home.

Wildlife has flourished as well. In 2023, more than 170 species of birds, 25 species of fish, 50 species of mammals, and 75 amphibian and reptile species live in the forest. That number includes 11 animal species synonymous with South Carolina such as the Carolina wren, spotted salamander, wild turkey, wood duck, whitetail deer and the eastern tiger swallowtail butterfly.

*The trees not only came back in the forest, so did wildlife*

About 20 species of concern, rare plants, fish, insects and birds, live in the forest, including five insect species new to science, and ten of South Carolina's endangered and threatened plant and animal species. Although no longer considered endangered, the relatively rare bald eagle is occasionally seen in the forest. Plant species that might be encountered on a stroll through the forest range from beautiful showy orchids to unusual insect-eating plants like the Venus flytrap.

Streams, although still carrying a heavy bed load of sediment from decades of exploitative farming practices, now run clear thanks to the many years of reforestation efforts. The terraces built in the 1930s by CCC and WPA workers to help slow the overland flow of stormwater and reduce erosion work in conjunction with decades of forest cover growth to slow run-off and allow precipitation to seep into ephemeral drainages and emerge as clear water that feeds into perennial streams. These streams now support dozens of fish species.

*Streams now run clear in the Clemson Experimental Forest*

Historical and cultural sites created by humans are also found in the forest. The home of Revolutionary War hero General Andrew Pickens, Hopewell plantation, as well as the ruins of other plantations, are within the tract. In addition, CCC and WPA structures and works, such as picnic shelters, bridges and roads dating back to the 1930s are protected here. The forest also serves as the home of the Clemson University Outdoor Lab, a university facility that provides a venue for meetings, camps, weddings and family reunions in a beautiful outdoor setting, as well as a camp for adults and children of varied abilities.

The Clemson Experimental Forest provides a wide range of habitats, from early successional stages when new stands of trees are regenerated, to mature stands of mixed hardwood species; from xeric upland sites to beaver-created wetlands; and riparian zones to upland ecotones between vegetative communities. Even manmade structures, like Issaqueena dam built by the WPA, add to the diversity of habitats and, when combined with other efforts of man and nature, support an outstanding diversity of plants and animals.

The forest is readily accessible with over 225 miles of roads and 100+ miles of trails, allowing students, faculty and the public to enjoy its many benefits; yet there are opportunities for solitude and individual sports like hunting and fishing here as well.

Presently 35 classes from various university departments use the forest as a classroom. It supports a broad range of research, including studies in forestry, wildlife management, environmental sustainability, biodiversity and carbon sequestration. Well over 400 publications have come from this research, including results from many doctoral and master's research projects. Almost all of them attest, in one way or the other, to the power of conservation in creating this magnificent and unique resource.

The Clemson Experimental Forest is certainly a testament to the power of conservation. Thanks to efforts beginning with a proposal to the federal government requesting the purchase of the eroded, submarginal farmland and the work of New Deal programs, the almost barren and eroded land was planted to pine and hardwood species, trails were created, structures and roads were built, and the farmland was transformed into the thriving forest it is today.

Decades of abuse had strained the ability of the land to support native plant species, wildlife and high-quality water. The Clemson Experimental Forest stands as a testament to the tenacity of nature, aided by the conservation efforts of man, in developing an area that is diverse and productive again.

Currently, no other university can match this magnificent 17,500-acre forest adjacent to the Clemson University campus. Protection of this treasure will help ensure that Clemson continues to be a leader in teaching, research, forest resources management, environmental sustainability and public service. The forest is to Clemson a treasure beyond measure.

But nature is also vulnerable. Conservation can create and maintain a forest but cannot fully stop efforts to nibble away at it through encroachment and fragmentation. Although the tenets of the Bankhead-Jones Act of 1939 theoretically protect the forest from these types of activities, they may not be enough in this age of uncontrolled urban and suburban sprawl. More protection is needed. By placing the forest in a conservation easement, the land would still be owned by Clemson University but could not be commercially developed. This easement would further protect the properties and help ensure the land would continue to be used for conservation, education and recreation, as intended in the original act.

# A DAY ON THE SOQUE

*David Van Lear*

For over 60 years, I have had the almost impossible goal of catching my dream trifecta: a 10-pound largemouth bass, a 10-pound brown trout and a 10-pound rainbow trout. This is a dream I have had since my earliest years growing up on the Cowpasture River in Virginia where I first became addicted to the joys of fishing. As a teenager I read the outdoor magazines like Sports Afield, Field and Stream and Outdoor Life which lit the torch in my mind of one day catching these dream fish. It took many years, but now in my mid-80s, I have finally achieved that goal.

I fulfilled the goal of catching a 10-pound largemouth bass in Florida in 1969 while I held a postdoctoral position at the University of Florida. On a return trip the next year, before the spawn, I caught a 10-pound, 6-ounce largemouth on a bullhead minnow in a small pond in the sandhills of north Florida.

The second part of my dream, catching a 10-pound brown trout, was fulfilled in the fall of 1984 when I caught an 8½-pound trout from Lake Jocassee. My friend Willy Williams netted the fish, and as we got it into my boat, the trout released all of her eggs. Being a fisherman, I wanted to ensure that I could count her maximum weight for bragging purposes. I looked online for the weight of eggs in a mature brown trout. When I saw "between two and three pounds," I did what any self-respecting angler would do: I added the weight of the eggs in calculating the weight of my fish, making her a 10-pound-plus brown trout. That trout was caught on a Rapala lure when the large browns in the lake were trying to move into tributaries to spawn in late October.

My third objective has proven the most difficult to fulfill, but now I can say I've done it! And it only took me 83 years to do it!

This conquest happened on November 6, 2023, when my friend Allen Weldon and I reserved a spot on the Soque River in north Georgia. This outing turned out to be one of the most enjoyable fishing experiences of my life.

We fished on a private stretch of the river — the owner owns more than a mile of the river, including the river bottom and its corridor, and "no trespassing" is strictly enforced. Fishing here is by reservation only. The river is stocked with trout, including palomino trout — a hybrid resulting from crossing rainbow trout and golden trout. The trout are fed on a frequent basis. As a result, the fish grow to amazing sizes.

I told Allen on our drive over from Clemson that I hoped to catch a three-pounder. That would make my day. He didn't tell me what his goal was. Allen is very experienced at fishing for bass and catfish but is a relative novice when it comes to fly fishing for trout.

We met a good friend of Allen's named John Salazar at the property owner's house on the river. John would be fishing with us. For our guide that day, we had hired a young man named Ricky who had been a guide on the river for several years. We could not have had a more competent guide.

Ricky led us down to the river shortly after noon. Even as we approached, we could see palomino trout swimming around in the part of the river we were going to fish. They were magnificent and from our vantage point looked to be about 18- to 25-inches long. There were rainbow trout there, too, but they were more difficult to see with their dark backs.

Ricky gave me a hand as we climbed down a rocky slope to get in the river. While my balance leaves a lot to be desired, he got me down safely. Allen and John followed, and we waded quietly across the river and spread out, as Ricky suggested.

I hooked a fish on my first cast, but it quickly pulled loose. I was using a #18 pheasant tail nymph. It seemed ridiculously small for the size of the trout we saw, but Ricky knew what he was doing, and I have learned over the years that you should do what your guide tells you. After a while, I hooked and landed a palomino trout. I'd estimate it was close to 25 inches long, and we guessed its weight to be about five pounds. It was a gorgeous fish with the red stripe of the rainbow trout down its flank and on its gill plates. The remainder of the fish was the golden color it inherited from the golden trout, a native of the Sierra Nevada mountains in California.

After a couple of hours, during which time I landed another palomino trout and several rainbows in the 16- to 18-inch range, I had a strike that I knew was something quite different. It was really heavy and strong. As soon as this fish struck, it raced upstream on the far side of the river and kept going for about 40 yards, making my reel scream as it ripped off the line. Then the huge fish jumped clear of the water — twice. I couldn't believe a fish that big could jump completely out of the water — like a steelhead, I thought — but it did.

*My big palomino trout caught on the Soque River*

As I struggled to maintain pressure and keep my rod tip up, the fish took off downstream. It streaked past me, jumped twice and just kept going. It must have been 50 yards downstream when it made its final two jumps, coming completely out of the water again. Suddenly my line stopped moving. The fish had hung up on a branch or rock far downstream. I was sure he would break off the line or pull the tiny nymph from its jaw.

*An estimated 10-pound rainbow trout from the Soque River*

Our guide, Ricky, saved the day. He quickly took my rod and waded across and downstream until he was beside the branch that was holding my trout. He worked his magic and somehow freed my line, then quickly waded back to give me the rod again. I was able to recover some line as the fish suddenly swam toward me, before he was off again on another downstream run. By now, I had been fighting this monster for approximately 15 minutes and my arm ached. I didn't know who was more worn out, me or the fish.

I gradually got the huge trout close enough for Ricky to net, and we both breathed a sigh of relief. We estimated the trout to weigh

10 pounds. Ricky said it was one of the largest rainbows that had been caught this year in the Soque. What a fish! I have caught sea-run rainbows, called steelhead, when I was a graduate student at the University of Idaho that weighed up to 17½ pounds, but they are in a different category from the non-anadromous strain of rainbow that I had just caught in the Soque River.

Ricky worked with the huge and exhausted rainbow for about five minutes to revive it. Finally, it was strong enough to swim on its own and with a tail splash it took off back into the river — leaving me with a memory to last the rest of my life.

Allen and John were having good luck, too. Allen caught two beautiful palomino trout and several rainbows. John caught a number of big rainbows (but not as big as mine — haha, John). They both were so helpful to this old man during his day of fishing and did not even tease me about forgetting to bring my waders when we left Clemson. My fishing day was saved because, thankfully, the owner of the property loaned me a pair of his extra waders.

What memories I will have of this day! Beautiful country, fall colors, good friends and memorable fish. It was such a great experience that I was inspired to send President Jimmy Carter an email describing our wonderful day. I knew he had fished the river many years earlier because we saw a huge picture of him fighting a big trout on the wall of the owner's house when we registered to fish. In the picture, he had a determined smile on his face as he fought "a big 'un."

Though as I write this, President Carter is 99 years old, in hospice care at his home in Plains, Georgia, and has just suffered the loss of his wife Rosalynn, we had shared a similar experience. I hoped my email and photos would bring him fond memories of his time on the Soque just as that day had created for me.

www.ingramcontent.com/pod-product-compliance
Lightning Source LLC
LaVergne TN
LVHW012023060526
838201LV00061B/4436